W9-AXL-520

Remington: The Complete Prints

ALSO BY PEGGY AND HAROLD SAMUELS

Illustrated Biographical Encyclopedia of Artists of the American West

Collected Writings of Frederic Remington

Frederic Remington, A Biography

Contemporary Western Artists

Everyone's Guide to Buying Art

Techniques of the Master Painters of the American West

REMINGTON
The Complete Prints

by Peggy and Harold Samuels

Crown Publishers, Inc., New York

Text that is referred to or quoted without giving another source is
from Peggy and Harold Samuels's *Frederic Remington, A Biography,*
Doubleday & Company, Inc., Garden City, New York, 1982,
reprinted by the University of Texas Press, Austin, Texas, 1985.

Copyright © 1990 by Peggy Samuels and Harold Samuels

All rights reserved. No part of this book may be reproduced or
transmitted in any form or by any means, electronic or mechanical,
including photocopying, recording, or by any information storage and
retrieval system, without permission in writing from the publisher.

Published by Crown Publishers, Inc., 201 East 50th Street,
New York, New York 10022

CROWN is a trademark of Crown Publishers, Inc.

Manufactured in Japan

LIBRARY OF CONGRESS CATALOGING-IN-PUBLICATION DATA

Samuels, Peggy.
Remington: the complete prints / by Peggy & Harold Samuels.
1. Remington, Frederic, 1861–1909—Catalogs.   2. Prints,
American—Catalogs.   3. Prints—19th century—United
States—Catalogs.
4. West (U.S.) in art—Catalogs.   I. Samuels, Harold.
II. Remington, Frederic, 1861–1909.   III. Title.
NE539.R46A4   1989
769.92—dc20   89-15740   CIP

ISBN 0-517-57451-9

10 9 8 7 6 5 4 3 2 1

First Edition

Contents

Foreword

Each week calls and letters come to the Frederic Remington Art Museum asking for information about the old Remington prints that were published by P. F. Collier & Son, R. H. Russell, *Harper's Weekly,* and others. Sometimes the individual only wants to know the title or the size of an image that he has, or the date completed. At other times the questions become more lengthy: Where was it published and what medium did he use? Is there an article that accompanies the piece and where can they see other similar prints? Occasionally the caller wonders whether his colored print might be an original watercolor or painting.

Until now there has never been a complete reference covering all of the known lifetime prints by Frederic Remington. Many of the 148 works shown in this book exist only in print form since the original was destroyed by the artist himself.

This work by Peggy and Harold Samuels will surely become an invaluable guide to the Western art collector, museums, and anyone interested in the work of this great American artist.

Lowell McAllister, Executive Director
Frederic Remington Art Museum
Ogdensburg, New York

Introduction

Frederic Remington's prints are now a hundred years old. They provide a wide-ranging record of the dangers and glories of the open prairies that once existed beyond the Mississippi, as well as a chronicle of savage conflicts between the Indians, the cavalry, and the frontiersmen. The stories Remington told in his paintings were so novel at the turn of the century that much of what the populous East knew about the romance of the West was learned from his art.

During Remington's career, he was characterized first as a realist and later as "an ideational and subjective synthesizer of harmony and mystery." After his premature death in late 1909, however, his reputation suffered. He was thought to have been only a cowboy artist, another Charley Russell. More recently, appreciation of his work

Figure 1. Remington rocking in his little chair. [Frederic Remington Art Museum]

has grown and spread beyond Westerners. Even Eastern art connoisseurs have accepted him as an American master.

Learned curators who used to claim that Remington's early demise was not a great loss because he would have contributed nothing new to art if he had lived now write that he was an American genius who would have had an even brighter artistic future. Leading modern critics who once boasted they could not be bribed to attend a Remington exhibition now report glowingly on the impressionism, tonalism, symbolism, aestheticism, and other praiseworthy -isms they find in his paintings being shown in major museums nationally.

Despite this new praise, though, the paintings chosen for current Remington exhibitions necessarily come up short in demonstrating the scope of his power because he deliberately burned more than a hundred of his paintings on four occasions near the end of his life. He believed they failed to meet the critical standards of the day.

Unfortunately, the works Remington set fire to included such masterpieces as *Bringing Home the New Cook* (plate 124), *Drifting Before the Storm* (plate 92), the sensitive trilogy *Tragedy of the Trees* (plates 117–120), all but one of *The Great American Explorers* series (plates 107, 108, 110–114), and *The Unknown Explorers* (plate 115). He also destroyed *The Buffalo Hunter* (plate 145), *The Warrior's Last Ride* (plate 128), *The Ceremony of the Scalps* (plate 126), *The Gathering of the Trappers* (plate 89), *The Santa Fe Trade* (plate 88), and *Forsythe's Fight on the Republican River* (plate 48). The present value of the paintings he burned would be many millions of dollars, but they exist now only in reproductions of the originals.

Other important paintings by Remington have simply disappeared over the years. Moreover, some owners of original Remingtons are unwilling to lend them to public exhibitions for fear of damage or robbery. As a consequence, as many as half of the pictures reproduced in this book are not available for exhibition today.

Another factor that limits the scope of original Remington paintings in current exhibitions is the selection process by museum curators who may be influenced by personal obligations to a particular institution, collector, or dealer. In contrast, the production of prints during Remington's lifetime was strictly a commercial venture by his publishers. Their choices were not filtered through expert tastes or professional relationships. Their decisions were never complicated by thoughts of whether a painting was considered "good art" in terms of the transient aesthetic guidelines of the era. Even Remington himself had little part in deciding which of his pictures were made into prints.

Rather, selection of what was to be reproduced as a print was based on what ordinary people liked enough to purchase, frame, and hang in their home. Reproductions cost from ten cents to two dollars, not two thousand dollars, the price of a major Remington painting then. Remington's prints were people's art. Hundreds of copies of each original painting were published. Paintings were for the few, prints for the many.

The critics of Remington's time as well as their modern counterparts state firmly, however, that the paintings the public should appreciate most are those he did in 1909, the last year of his life. Regrettably, the paintings he produced then were not made into prints because his publisher, *Collier's* magazine, canceled his contract in 1908. The cancellation was due primarily to the editors' dissatisfaction with the fashionable turn of his art.

One painting typical of his work in 1909 is a nocturne in blue tones featuring the familiar device of a full moon on the horizon at left. Centered is a mounted Indian sentinel facing the viewer, immobile. The colors are lovely, but all of the excitement and vigor of earlier Remingtons is gone. There is no structure, no story, even though the theme was one he had painted a score of times when he used a more vibrant palette, a stronger composition, and figures that at least hinted at action or drama, past or to come (see plate 125).

This static nocturne is an abrupt change from the dynamism Remington evidenced in his paintings that were made into prints. It is difficult to imagine this massive man at the end of his abbreviated career, rocking on his little studio chair (fig. 1) while dabbing the canvas with pastel dots and dashes like a message in Morse code sent to appease critics vigilantly on guard against narration on canvas. His goal in 1909 seemed to be the acme of bland.

Compare this nocturne to paintings done earlier and made into prints. *His First Lesson* (plate 84) was painted in 1903, when Remington's earth tones and brushwork were already characteristic of his brand of Impressionism. The sliver of blue sky appears dynamic when weighed against the shadow of the fence rail on the earth. The background is composed of static squares, heightening the tension of the event taking place in the foreground. The slight gestures of the two men gingerly training the skeptical young mustang imply violent action. The backdrop is so still that the figures seem to leap off the canvas.

Remington wanted to burn the original of *His First Lesson* merely because it told a story and thus did not meet the standard that ultimately governed his critical and personal approach to art. Yet his public loved the print, which was issued and reissued and then offered in portfolios. Because he had already sold the painting before he started burning canvases, *His First Lesson* survived and is universally recognized as a masterpiece.

In contrast to the whimsical tale told in *His First Lesson, Downing the Nigh Leader* (plate 122) displays a different facet of Remington's talent. This painting is a prime example of his use of overt sequential happenings. The desperate progression of the actors is from right to left across the canvas, while the story reads from left to right.

The Indian towering over his galloping little pony has driven a lance into the jaw of the falling leader on the driver's left. The right leader is being dragged to the side and will be down in a matter of seconds. The horse behind him is leaping onto his back, while the black and white head behind the left leader looks like a symbolic skull. There is no hope. The front wheel of the coach is turning in. The episode will be over in less than a minute, the horses falling in a jumble and the coach overturned. All of the white characters are at the mercy of the implacable Indians.

While Remington was still alive, the humorous *His First Lesson* and the dramatic *Downing the Nigh Leader* were selected by consensus as pictures people wanted to have in their homes. There is no reason to suppose that the choice of today's public would be different.

The 148 prints collected here allow a picture-by-picture evaluation of twenty-one years of Remington's progress as an artist, skipping only 1886–87 when he was the new boy finding his way, and 1909 when he was adrift in symbolism, without a publisher. They provide an informal retrospective of the best of his work from 1888 to 1908 that cannot be duplicated.

Almost all of the prints are reproductions carefully made from the original printing plates. They were photographed from paintings just as illustrations in an exhibition catalog are. For the many paintings that no longer exist or are not available, these prints are the only memorials of Remington's work. They are irreplaceable fine-art reproductions as well as highly collectible and affordable Americana. They will never be worth less than they are now.

Except for *A Dash for the Timber* (plate 15), *The Sentinel* (plate 134), and *The Last of His Race* (plate 127), the prints were first published with text in magazines, books, and portfolios. They are listed here chronologically by the date of first appearance. This is the only practical method of organization because many prints were not otherwise dated and some prints were dated two or three different times as they were republished.

The Young Illustrator

Right from his oversized entry into the world, Frederic Remington was a character larger than life. Strangers had clear memories of him as a child. When he was a youth, people who had never met him saved his clever letters and crude drawings. As a man, he had a hundred male friends and three female friends. He knew people in every walk of life, the rich and famous and powerful in the East, as well as some ordinary folk in the West.

He was exasperatingly hyperactive when he was growing up in the North Country of New York State, where he was born October 4, 1861. An only child, he had the heavy frame of his placid mother (fig. 2) rather than the slenderness of his father, whose dash he would have preferred. His father was a legitimate Civil War hero, a colonel in the

Figure 2. Remington as a
child standing beside his
mother. [Frederic Remington
Art Museum]

Figure 3. The central figure is
Remington's father, the war
hero. [Frederic Remington
Art Museum]

United States Volunteer Cavalry (fig. 3). He instilled in Remington a love of horses and an admiration for the military.

As a young man, Remington leaned toward art as a career although he demonstrated little talent for sketching. There was no background of art in his home or in his village. His parents considered painting to be only a pastime for women, but they indulged his request to go to Yale Art School in September 1878. If there had been the most elementary entrance examination, he could not have passed.

Yale dampened his desire to be a painter. He detested drawing from plaster casts and instead specialized in playing football. After going home for Christmas in 1879, he never returned to school in New Haven. There is no indication his art benefited in any way from his brief encounter with strict classical training.

From then on Remington drifted. The longest he stuck to anything was two years. He worked as a government clerk in Albany until 1882, spent ten months as a "holiday" sheepman in Kansas, and a year and a half in Kansas City, Missouri, where his new wife left him because he hid from her his part ownership of a failing saloon.

His early Western experiences were limited to the unproductive Kansas venture and a vacation trip to Montana in August 1881, when he sold *Harper's Weekly* a cowboy sketch (fig. 4) so rough it had to be redrawn by a staff artist.

In September 1885 he moved to Brooklyn, New York, where his wife joined him. They were supported by his father's brother while he made the rounds of publishers, looking for work as an illustrator of Western subjects. To promote himself he dressed "like a cowboy just off a ranch" and showed his unpolished Western sketches that nevertheless had the "ring of live material."

After *Harper's Weekly* bought two more sketches, his uncle paid five dollars a month in tuition for Remington to enter the Art Students League in New York City on March 1, 1886. At the League he was exposed to professional illustrators for the first time. He watched their methods, yet he still could not draw a satisfactory human figure. Physically he was the strongest man studying at the League, overpowering the future superstar illustrator Charles Dana Gibson in arm wrestling, but he was far from the strongest draftsman. Another sketch he sold *Harper's Weekly* also had to be redrawn.

When the school term ended on May 29, Remington never went back. Three days after the League closed for the summer, he was on a train heading west into Arizona. *Harper's Weekly* had commissioned him to report on the army's arduous search for the Apache chief Geronimo, who had left the reservation to take to the warpath.

With his customary prudence, Remington changed the assignment from chasing Geronimo to the more mundane title he chose, "Soldiering in the Southwest." His credentials as a *Harper's* correspondent let him fraternize with Generals Nelson Miles (plates 30–43) and George Forsyth (plate 48), who later figured in his career. He transformed obscure Lieutenant Powhatan Clarke into a hero like his father to provide exciting copy for *Harper's*. At twenty-four and an artist for less than a year, Remington was already acting like the luminary he was soon to be.

Most of Remington's baggage on the trip west was photographic gear. He used the word *sketch* to cover both pencil drawings and photographs, and he took more pictures than he drew. When he returned to Brooklyn on June 29, 1886, he improved his draftsmanship by copying his own photographs and other photographs he bought during the trip. Duplicating these images for *Harper's Weekly* and *Outing* magazine was his real schooling, and he was able to earn while he learned.

In a short time his hand became so sure that illustrations took him hours rather than days, and he pressed *Harper's* for more assignments. In his first half year as an illustrator, magazines purchased twenty-five of his drawings. He had found his life's work. He bragged to a friend out West, "That's a pretty good break for an ex cow-puncher to come to New York with $30 and catch on in 'art.' " He embodied the cowboy for his New York friends. His speech was laconic. His vocabulary was small, vital, and picturesque. He was tall for the day and heavy, round faced, smooth shaven.

Remington continued to progress rapidly in illustrative technique. Within months he taught himself to use photographs only as a starting point rather than as images to imitate. Nonetheless, art scholars still criticized him for copying. They compared his galloping horses with horses in newly available stop-action photographs. Horse trainers were equally disconcerted by Remington's depiction of the gallop. They said no normal horse could achieve the extended positions Remington drew.

The public was not confused by the criticism, despite their lack of understanding of the kinetics of the gallop. Remington's horses appeared to be running faster than the horses in photographs. People knew instinctively that in a race, his horses would win. The explanation was that in drawing his horses, Remington went beyond photographic realism to create a look of greater speed and urgency (plate 142).

Remington's first major assignment came in 1887, when he was asked to draw eighty-three illustrations for Theodore Roosevelt's *Ranch Life and the Hunting Trail.* Deprecators claimed Remington "was lucky to stumble on a new field, the West," but there had been

Figure 4. Remington sold *Harper's Weekly* a sketch. [Authors' collection]

dozens of artists across the Mississippi before him. His triumph was in accentuating realism with a "coolly appraising American eye." In contrast with most of his competitors, he drew Mexicans, Indians, and black cavalrymen without prejudice.

He entered one of his oil paintings in the prestigious annual exhibition of the National Academy of Design in March 1888. The *New York Herald* recognized immediately that he would "one day be listed among our great American painters." He was acknowledged to be one of the country's leading young artists, forced to illustrate simply because American paintings of American subjects were not selling well enough to provide an income he would accept. Other critics, however, called his Indians "caricatures."

In August 1888 he wrote and illustrated an article for *Century* as an expert on American horses. His prospects were bright and his earnings were high. When his first four prints were published in John Muir's series of portfolios *Picturesque California,* Remington was a highly regarded professional illustrator of Western genre subjects. To supplement the work of the more famous painters Thomas Moran, Thomas Hill, and William Keith, who did landscapes, Remington concentrated on human and animal figures. He was able to hold his own in creating these technically advanced photogravures. The only disturbing note in the Muir portfolios was the spelling of his given name with an added *k,* an error Remington hated all his life because he believed it made him appear to be German.

Remington was making his mark by depicting horses, so he led with horses and mules as the subjects of *Mule Train Crossing the Sierras,* the first Muir print (plate 1). The picture was a pure illustration of Muir's text, not fine art, but the excellence of the drawn figures overcame their passivity and the crowded composition. He began in 1888 with figures at rest, the same way he concluded in 1909.

The third and fourth Muir prints (plates 3 and 4) continued to show serenity and excellent draftsmanship, but the second, *Branding Cattle* (plate 2), was poorly drawn. The figures were not in proportion and the focus was lost. Remington did not have to do the work over only because the publisher faced a deadline

in San Francisco while the artist was in New York City.

The two sporting prints, *Antelope Hunting* (plate 7) and *Goose Shooting* (plate 8), were chromolithographs, not photographic reproductions. For these two prints, Remington's original paintings were copied onto treated "stones" by craftsmen. There may have been as many as forty stones involved, one for each color, tint, and shade. Problems with focus and the nineteenth-century feeling of the compositions are attributable to the artist, but the poor draftsmanship of the prone figures could have been a craftsman's fault.

Instead of concentrating on prints, Remington continued to look for a role in fine art. In 1889 he submitted a painting to the Paris International Exhibition and won a medal. There was little income to be earned from fine art or from prints, though, while illustrating was making him a rich man. His wife said, "He has all he can do. Fred is told by artists that he is talked about more than any artist in this country."

On December 3, 1888, Mrs. Remington wrote, "Fred has just left for Boston. He goes to see Houghton, Mifflin about illustrating 'Hiawatha.' Ever since he has done any illustrating he has dreamed about that. Fred is as busy as a bee and very happy." The 22 black-and-white paintings and 379 pen-and-ink sketches for "Hiawatha" (plates 9–12) were truly his dream assignment, but he had so much work to complete first that he could not start until the summer of 1889.

During the summer, he sat in a skiff on a mountain lake, his drawing board balanced on the sides. Other days he would place his easel near a stump on the shore. "He'd sit there cross-legged painting, diddling his free foot up and down and whistling until we thought we would go mad."

Remington looked on the "Hiawatha" illustrations merely as decorations. He insisted on a printed notice that he had followed the poet in freedom of treatment. Nevertheless, he was criticized because "he dressed the ancient Ojibwa in nineteenth-century clothing."

The next year, 1890, Remington began to involve himself in the brand-new halftone photoengraving process for reproducing his pictures in books, magazines, and as prints. With the process in mind, he painted in black and white, adding accents of color to enliven the painting when it was reproduced. *Harper's Weekly* was so pleased that *An Army Mail Ambulance* was run as a double-page supplement in sepia (plate 13). This was at last the real Remington where he skillfully presented a characteristically exciting episode that suggested a story.

In contrast, *On the Cattle Range* (plate 14) was a naïve depiction of man bites dog, almost the equivalent of a folksy rendition by Charley Russell. Like *An Army Mail Ambulance,* this print was not strictly an illustration. Although it was painted for *Harper's Weekly,* the text came later, supplementing the picture.

A Dash for the Timber (plate 15) was a huge easel painting done in full color for a private commission. Because Remington was not pressed for time, he was able to ask friends in the Southwest to send him cowboy garb so he could draw authentically dressed figures. He entered the painting in the autumn 1889 National Academy exhibition and was gratified when critics declared that it "marks an advance of one of the strongest of our young artists."

The picture was enhanced by its evocative title, which was dramatic enough for a short story, whereas other artists might have settled for *Indians Chasing Cowboys.* With its high action and massed horses in broad daylight, *A Dash for the Timber* was the pick of these early prints. Because chromolithographs like *Antelope Hunting* were expensive and colored photographic reproductions were not yet feasible technically, printmakers solicited Remington for the right to publish black-and-white or sepia reproductions of full-color paintings, as they did with *A Dash for the Timber.*

By May 1890, *Harper's* had launched a promotional campaign depicting Remington as both a rough-hewn Westerner and a scholar who "draws what he knows and knows what he draws." His substantial earnings enabled him to buy an estate in suburban New Rochelle, New York. Always a massive eater and heavy drinker, he now weighed 230 pounds.

On the March—The Advance Guard (plate 16) precedes the Werner prints of 1898 (plates 30–43) in relating General Nelson Miles's experiences at the head of the Indian-fighting army. At first glance it seems odd that a print would be made of such an ordinary subject as cavalry marching, but the subject is a warm look at a routine Remington loved.

A Fantasy from the Pony War Dance (plate 17) is a print that collectors talk about but none owns. The one recorded surviving example was stolen from a private home in 1986 and has not surfaced since then.

A Russian Cossack (plate 18) anticipates the 1909 paintings. Remington was already using Impressionist colors to depict passive subjects by the time of his 1892 European trip, which included visits to Parisian galleries. Then he retrogressed. In the course of another decade of mostly black-and-white commercial work, he lost confidence for a while in his ability to see and duplicate color.

Friends in the cavalry told him the maneuver in *Moving the Led Horses* (plate 19) must have come from his European experiences because headstrong American mustangs could never be held alongside each other in that parade-ground manner. The painting is also an early example of a Remington idiosyncrasy. To illustrate an 1893 article about General George Custer, Remington chose a view from the rear of the fighting, not from the front line. Five years later, in his famous article on the Spanish-American War, "With the Fifth Corps," the action was again shown from the rear of the battle (plate 46).

In the cavalry picture, the horses form a V aimed at the viewer rather than the more usual sweeping line of riders as in *A Dash for the Timber* and the crowded *Sioux Indians Charging the Sun-Pole* (plate 20).

1.

Mule Train Crossing the Sierras

1888. "During the exciting times that followed the discovery of gold near Mono Lake, it frequently became a matter of considerable pecuniary importance to force a way through the canyon with [a] pack-train early in the spring."—Muir, page 24 [Amon Carter Museum]

2.

Branding Cattle (An Incident of Ranch Life)

1888. "The settlers [in Southern California] were from Spain or Mexico, of pure white blood and good family. They were given grants made large to support the immense herds of cattle necessary for profit when hides and tallow were the only income."
—Muir, page 191
[Authors' collection]

3.
Miners Prospecting for Gold

1888. "Gold had been washed from mountains by centuries of attrition to where it was found by farmers and mill hands of General Sutter. Having found these particles, they searched in similar places, till finally they pursued it up the mountains."
—Muir, page 233
[The Library of Congress]

4.
A Navaho Sheep-Herder

1888. This photogravure is in section seven of the portfolio, where Muir's attention turned to the mountain states. There is no specific reference to the Navaho sheepherder, so Remington was working from his own observations in the Southwest.
[Amon Carter Museum]

5.

A Bucking Bronco

1888. Illustrating the
Roosevelt book was Remington's first big job. The nega-
tive of the figures in the
illustration was stamped in
gold on the book's cover,
deleting the landscape. To
break up the heavy gold
panel in the lower right,
the hat was moved down
from upper right.

[The Library of Congress]

6.

Dragging a Bull's Hide
over a Prairie Fire in
Northern Texas

1888. "Mr. Remington in his
realistic sketch shows how,
when there is a strain on the
rope, the cow-boy always
throws himself to the opposite side. Mr. Remington pic-
torially puts exact conditions
before readers, and supplements them by writing."
—*Harper's Weekly,*
10/27/1888, page 815
[Authors' collection]

7.

Antelope Hunting

1889. "Arriving where nearer approach mounted would alarm the game, the ranchman ran stooping and finally crept stealthlly to the ledge, where he peered cautiously above the edge and saw the antelope. A quick, but careful aim, and the rifle cracked."
—Gould, (unpaged)
[Authors' collection]

8.

Goose Shooting, a.k.a.
Canada Goose Shooting,
a.k.a. Pheasant Shooting

1889. "I was staying last fall with a farmer who was the owner of live geese decoys. These we would anchor in the Platte. My host had a mongrel called a 'spanell,' and I pitied the brute when on some cold day he was to retrieve a goose or duck."
—Gould, (unpaged)
[Authors' collection]

9.

Hiawatha and the Pearl-Feather, a.k.a. An Indian Battle

1890. This was the all-day fight of Hiawatha (on the left) and Pearl-Feather, "the mighty,/Tall of stature, broad of shoulder,/Dark and terrible in aspect,/Clad from head to foot in wampum,/Armed with all his weapons."
—Longfellow, page 89
[The Library of Congress]

10.

Hiawatha's Wedding Feast, a.k.a. An Indian Dance

1890. "Then Old Nokomis said, 'O Pau-Puk-Keewis,/ Dance for us,/That the feast may be more joyous.' He was dressed in doeskin fringed with ermine. On his head were plumes of swan's down. On his heels were tails of foxes."—Longfellow, page 109
[The Library of Congress]

11.
Picture-Writing
1890. "Said Hiawatha, 'Lo!
how all things fade!'/From
his pouch he took colors,/
On the smooth bark of a
birch-tree/Painted many
shapes and figures,/And
each figure had a meaning./
All these did
Hiawatha/Show unto his
people."—Longfellow,
page 142
[The Library of Congress]

12.
The Hunting of
Pau-Puk-Keewis, a.k.a.
An Indian Runner
1890. "Full of wrath was Hia
watha./Hard his breath came
through his nostrils./'I will
slay this Pau-Puk-Keewis.'/
Then in swift pursuit
departed/Hiawatha and the
hunters. Over rock and river/
Ran cunning Pau-Puk-
Keewis."—Longfellow,
page 170
[The Library of Congress]

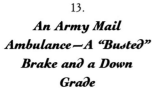

13.

**An Army Mail
Ambulance—A "Busted"
Brake and a Down
Grade**

1890. " 'How did that team
get down that mountain
side?' was asked Mr. Remington. 'I am sure I don't know'
was the artist's reply. 'What I
was most intent on was to
catch some of the points for a
sketch. I was on the seat with
the driver.' "—*Harper's
Weekly,* 9/20/1890, page 742
[Authors' collection]

14.

**On the Cattle
Range—"What's the
Show for a Christmas
Dinner, Chief?"**

1890. "Dick came within
sight of the Sioux Reservation. He made his request in
plain English. Dick found the
meat to be tender and well
flavored. He inquired by
signs what it was. The Indian
host bobbed his head. 'Bow-
wow-wow, yap-yap,' he said."
—*Harper's Weekly,*
12/20/1890, page 990
[Authors' collection]

15.

A Dash for the Timber

1890. Remington showed the painting at the 1889 National Academy exhibition. *The Times* observed that it was "the picture before which stand the largest number of people," adding that "the white men are the types in grogshops or among bummers or in prisons." [The Gund Collection of Western Art]

16.

On the March—The Advance Guard, a.k.a. Advance Guard

1891. On August 11, 1877, General Miles sent the Seventh Cavalry to the Upper Yellowstone to capture the Nez Percés led by Chief Joseph. At first Joseph outstripped his pursuers, but Miles's main force caught up and attacked. Joseph had not guarded his flank. [The Library of Congress]

17.

A Fantasy from the Pony War Dance

1891. Julian Ralph described how Remington and he "chartered" the Blackfoot nation for two days and concluded, "It was as if we had seen the ghosts of a dead people ride back to parody scenes in an era that had vanished.—*Harper's Monthly* 12/1891, page 39. This print is rare in color. [Authors' collection, tear sheet]

18.

A Russian Cossack

1892. "To illustrate the originality of the American illustrator, take Frederic Remington. Here is a man who is so jealous of it [his originality] that only within a year has he consented to go abroad for fear of weakening it."—Smith, (unpaged) [Authors' collection]

19.

Moving the Led Horses,
a.k.a. Dismounted—The
Fourth Troopers Moving
the Led Horses

1893. Wood engraving. The
painting was originally used
as an illustration in "Custer's
Last Battle" in *Century:* "I
dismounted my men to fight
on foot. The led horses were
sent to the main command.
Every body now lay down
and spread himself out as
thin as possible."
—*The Century Magazine,*
1/1892, page 376
[Authors' collection]

20.

Sioux Indians Charging the Sun-pole, a.k.a. The Charge on the Sun-pole

1893. Wood engraving. "When medicine-men set the day, maidens strip the tree of its limbs. Before the sun rose, warriors faced the sun-pole. When the morning sun ap-peared, the medicine-man hurled forth a yell. The sun sent commands to its warriors on earth to charge."
—*The Century Magazine,* 3/1890, page 755
[The Thomas Gilcrease Institute of American History and Art]

The Star

Cow Pony Pathos
(plate 25, detail)

In the field, Remington was described by a cavalry officer as "a fat citizen. Smoothed over his closely shaven head was a soft little hat rolled up so as not to convey the impression you get from the head of a Japanese priest. A brown canvas hunting coat of generous proportions extended laterally, with gentle downward slope to the front and rear. A big good-natured overgrown boy you could not fail to like the first time you saw him."

In New York City he was a more urbane celebrity, mingling with the art and literary crowd at his club, The Players. His friends boasted that he was "a man among men, a deuce of a good fellow, he never drew but two women in his life, and they were failures." Indian women did not count.

He rewrote his biography to fit his new image, falsely alleging that he had helped to invent modern football, was intercollegiate boxing champ, served as confidential clerk to the governor of New York, punched cows in Montana for four years as a bona fide cowboy, made a good thing out of a Kansas mule ranch, wandered south as an Indian scout until he "dropped his wad," then took his drawings to *Harper's* and was instantly an artist. His livestock in Kansas had really been sheep, but he referred to them as mules because otherwise they might elicit an authentic cowman's contempt.

In this period immediately before the Spanish-American War, Remington painted as obsessively as he ate and drank. He claimed, "My drawing is done entirely from memory. I never use a camera now. The interesting never occurs in nature as a whole, but in pieces. It's more what I leave out than what I add." This was one of the first significant transitional stages in Remington's artistic progress. Major technical improvements had occurred, and the seeds of advances to come could be recognized.

A Running Bucker and *A "Sunfisher"* (plates 22 and 23) are similar to *A Bucking Bronco* (plate 5) in composition, but they show the sophistication achieved over seven years. The landscape was deleted to simplify the focus. The rider cuts a more romantic figure, dressed stylishly in jacket and chaps rather than in work clothes. He could be the same man, but he is more relaxed, in control of the bronco despite the twist of the mustang's body that gives it extra power.

At this time Remington was berating his friend Owen Wister for writing about cowboys as Anglo-Saxon in origin. The range riders were really from Mexico and Texas, he complained. When Remington drew these bronco busters, though, he made them Anglos, too, the better to please his own Anglo public.

Along with the transition in his style, his signature had shifted from "Frederic Remington" to "F. Remington," and from all capitals to capitals and lowercase. Finally he settled on the mature form, a firmly scripted "Frederic Remington" generally placed in the lower right corner of a horizontal painting.

His steady progress was a body blow to his competitors. His work had been more evocative of the picturesque West than theirs in 1888 when his first prints were published. By 1895 he had clearly outstripped other illustrators of the same subjects.

The next six prints (plates 24–29) were reproduced about 1897 from Remington's book *Drawings*, published by R. H. Russell. They are not illustrations. They do not illuminate a text, but they do tell simple, easily understood stories. The animals are treated sympathetically, arousing such basic emotions that the pictures were reduced to clichés after being copied by many other artists and cinematographers. The lone buffalo (plate 28), haunted by the skull of its ancestor and dwarfed by the immense empty landscape, symbolizes the end of the Old West.

The compositions are still realistic and busy. Yet the path that Remington's technique will take is clear. *A Misdeal* (plate 27) prepares the way for the more exciting and colorful but simplified *The Quarrel* (plate 131).

The prints from illustrations in General Nelson Miles's book *Personal Recollections* (plates 30–43) are 16″ x 24″, close to the size of the original black-and-white paintings. This is almost ten times larger than the reproductions in the general's book, where the compositions seemed to be crowded with excessive detail. Remington was packing maximum melodrama into a small space to try to satisfy a general who expected his book and Remington's illustrations to help him become president of the United States.

Although these Miles illustrations are unimpressive in the book, the prints are breathtaking in the larger size. They educated Easterners who had no other source of information about the hardships and successes in the campaigns of the Indian-fighting army. Remington knew the territory and the participants. Although he did not see the actual struggles, he based his interpretations on eyewitness accounts and on Miles's text that is quoted in the captions.

In addition, the prints provide some insight into Remington the man. In *Soldiers Opening Their Own Veins for Want of Water* (plate 31), he is at his most gruesome. This picture sets the stage for paintings of Indian rituals that he could not sell because his patrons said the figures were engaged in inhumane practices. In contrast, he indicates in *Indian Village Routed* (plate 32) his silent objection to the cruelty of cavalry charges on tepee villages. The Indian woman and child running last will be the first endangered by the troopers.

During this period, Remington was in his studio seven days a week, painting and sculpting. *Harper's* said he was the busiest artist in America. "Cowboys are cash with me," he admitted, although he really preferred to paint soldiers. He visited ranches and reservations in the West only to refresh himself on subject matter. He went happily to Montana, however, to be with the Tenth Cavalry.

He was named an associate member of the National Academy in 1891, but he suspended exhibiting there in 1895 because he was told he would never be elected to full membership. He was not popular with most of the artists who belonged to the Academy. He was too famous, too rich, too cocky, too ostentatious in his life style ever to be elected to full membership by his jealous peers. It was also true that his technique was not maturing quickly enough to satisfy the fine-art critics. His approach remained too realistic for the changing times, and his colors were too vivid.

In 1897, he leapt at the chance to report on a foreign war. He went to Cuba with correspondent Richard Harding Davis for Hearst's *Journal*, but he was disappointed. The legend is that he cabled Hearst, "There will be no war. I wish to return." Hearst allegedly replied, "You furnish the pictures and I'll furnish the war." Remington left Cuba anyhow.

The following year he attained his greatest public exposure. The United States Post Office selected two

Figure 5. He was blowing smoke. [Frederic Remington Art Museum]

paintings from *Drawings* for reproduction as stamps and issued 3.5 million of these little Remington "prints."

For a Kodak advertisement, the artist was photographed with derby, topcoat, and a carefully tended, short-lived flat mustache. He was blowing smoke from a cigarette in his left hand, and he held one glove and a cane in his right hand (fig. 5).

21.
Mounting a Wild One
1894. This oversized print
was of an illustration in an
article Remington wrote
about a rodeo he witnessed at
a Mexican ranch, Los Ojos:
When the *vaquero* mounts his
horse "all men must bow and
call him master."
[Authors' collection,
tear sheet]

22.
A Running Bucker
1895. The print is so fine that
it can be confused with an
original drawing. The picture
was reprinted in 1897 in
Remington's *Drawings,* but
it was flopped with the
horse's head to the left, so
a different signature had
to be substituted.
[Richard F. Brush Art Gallery, St. Lawrence University]

23.
A "Sunfisher"

1895. Bucking is instinctive in a wild horse. A running bucker dislodges its rider by leaping up, then hitting the ground with impact. A sunfisher spins as well, twisting in midair until the rider jumps off because he expects the horse to fall on its side. [The Thomas Gilcrease Institute of American History and Art]

24.
An Indian Soldier

1897. The 1896 agreement between R. H. Russell and Remington for the publication of *Drawings* provided for a deluxe edition of 250 copies, "it being understood Remington will sign each book together with a proof for each book."
[Amon Carter Museum]

The Indian Soldier.

25.
Cow Pony Pathos

1897. Which was the signed proof included in the deluxe edition of *Drawings*? There were two: *An Indian Soldier* and *Cow Pony Pathos*. The price was ten dollars for the edition bound in suede calfskin, signed, and in a box with the signed proof.
[Amon Carter Museum]

26.
An Overland Station—Indians Coming in with the Stage, a.k.a. An Attack on an Overland Coach
1897. Russell's retail price for platinum prints was ten dollars. He paid Remington a generous "50% royalty on the net jobbing price, five dollars, of copies sold of such reproductions." There is no record of a royalty for Remington on prints by other publishers.
[Amon Carter Museum]

27.
A Misdeal, a.k.a. A Miss Deal
1897. This type of violent scene became stereotyped in later paintings by Remington's followers and in Western movies. For Remington, however, cowboy gunplay was an infrequent subject at this midpoint in his career.
[Amon Carter Museum]

28.
Solitude

1897. The solitary miniature buffalo represents the disappearing Old West. The pathetic animal is depressed further by the presence of the ominous skull of one of its own ancestors in the otherwise barren surroundings.
[The Thomas Gilcrease Institute of American History and Art]

29.
A Citadel on the Plains

1897. Publisher R. H. Russell dipped generously into *Drawings* for his print supply. How many he used is a matter of conjecture, but it was at least a dozen from 1897 to 1900. Most of the prints bore his copyright.
[The Thomas Gilcrease Institute of American History and Art]

30.

Sioux Warriors, a.k.a.
The Attack

1898. Remington complained,
"This is a bad business—The
Werner Co are using my illustrations for Miles book. I
am going to jump them some
how—I think I shall sue for
drawings not returned,"
but he did not have
grounds to sue.
[The Rockwell Museum]

31.

Soldiers Opening Their Own Veins for Want of Water, a.k.a. *After the Skirmish*

1898. The "Miles book" Remington referred to above is *Personal Recollections of General Nelson A. Miles:* "The heat and absence of water caused intense suffering. Some of the men resorted to opening the veins and moistening their lips with their own blood."
—Miles, page 168
[The Rockwell Museum]

32.

Indian Village Routed, a.k.a. *Troop Surprising a Camp*

1898. "The Indians being driven upon the Llano Estacado, it was impossible to follow. Enough had been accomplished to demonstrate we were strong enough to successfully encounter any Indians in the field, but their subjugation would require time."—Miles, page 170
[The Rockwell Museum]

33.
**Twenty-five to One,
a.k.a. The Last Stand**

1898. "Six men were surrounded by 125 Kiowas and Comanches. At the first attack four were struck. Outnumbered 25 to 1, this little party defended their lives. They killed double their number. The Indians abandoned the attack at dark."
—Miles, page 173
[The Rockwell Museum]

34.
**General Miles Envoy to
the Hostiles on the
Staked Plains, a.k.a.
Indian Winter
Encampment on the
Staked Plain, a.k.a.
When Winter Is Cruel**

1898. "In January [1875], I sent a message carried by friendly Indians. They found the hostile camp on the border of New Mexico. The whole body commenced to move the two hundred miles to their agency, where they surrendered."
—Miles, page 176
[The Thomas Gilcrease Institute of American History and Art]

35.

Meeting Between the Lines, a.k.a. **The Parley**

1898. "Sitting Bull was told he could not be allowed to send out war parties. He said the white man never lived who loved an Indian and no true Indian did not hate the white man. I was convinced that more than talk would be required."—Miles, page 226 [The Rockwell Museum]

36.
Indians Firing the Prairie, a.k.a. Burning a Refuge

1898. Sitting Bull "and the men who accompanied him returned to their lines, calling out to prepare for battle. I ordered an advance and the Indians commenced setting fire to the dry prairie grass around the command, with other hostility."
—Miles, page 227
[The Rockwell Museum]

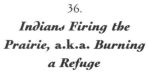

37.
Pursuing the Indians, a.k.a. Guarding the Supply Train

1898. "The energy of [our] attack and the persistence of the pursuit created such consternation in their camp that, after a pursuit of 42 miles, the Indians sent out another flag of truce and again requested an interview.
—Miles, page 228
[The Rockwell Museum]

38.

Captain Baldwin Hunting the Hostile Camp, a.k.a. _Hunting the Hostile Camp,_ a.k.a. _Scouting Party_

1898. "In order to reconnoitre, the command was divided into three columns, the third under Baldwin. He succeeded in striking Sitting Bull's camp at the head of the Red Water, where [we] captured his camp equipage and some horses."
—Miles, page 229
[The Rockwell Museum]

39.

**The Crazy Horse Fight,
a.k.a. *Attacking the
Indian Chief, "Crazy
Horse"***

1898. "The command deployed to attack warriors led by Crazy Horse, Little Big Man, and other chiefs of the Cheyennes and Ogalallas. The Indians called to the troops, 'You have had your last breakfast.' The snowstorm added weirdness."
—Miles, page 237
[The Rockwell Museum]

40.

The Lame Deer Fight

1898. "I extended my hand to Lame Deer. Unfortunately one of our white scouts covered the Indian. Lame Deer thought the scout was going to shoot. He raised his rifle and fired. I whirled my horse; the bullet killing a soldier near my side."
—Miles, page 248
[The Rockwell Museum]

41.
Mounting the Infantry on Captured Ponies

1898. "War ponies were selected with which to mount our foot-troops with Indian saddles. The man would reach his place whereupon the pony would make a bound into the air, coming down stiff-legged. The soldier's hat would fall and he would follow."
—Miles, page 252
[The Rockwell Museum]

42.
Fighting over the Captured Herd, a.k.a. *Fighting Over a Stolen Herd*, a.k.a. *Protecting the Herd*

1898. "As the Second Cavalry swept down the valley, Captain Tyler captured 300 ponies; Lieutenant Jerome, another large bunch; and Lieutenant McClernand secured 300 more. The Indians made several counter attacks, which were repelled."
—Miles, page 273
[The Rockwell Museum]

43.

Surrender of Chief
Joseph,* a.k.a.** ***The Truce
1898. "General Howard came
up and was present next
morning at the surrender of
Chief Joseph."—Miles, page
275. The Miles book also included a fifteenth Remington
illustration, *Lawton's Pursuit*
of Geronimo, which was not
included in the folder. It did
not glorify Miles.
[The Rockwell Museum]

The Maturing Process

I Will Tell the White Man How He Can Have His Ponies Back
(plate 55, detail)

In 1898, Remington went back to Cuba with the United States Fifth Army Corps to report on the Spanish-American War. He had a terrible time. He could not find the front of the battle of San Juan and saw the action from a thousand yards in the rear. Fever combined with his obesity made him a casualty of the tropical heat.

Another correspondent wrote sarcastically that Remington "left on Cuban soil as much of his flesh [through sweat] as a man who had lost a leg. For a campaign through wine country dotted with hotels, he was the best equipped war artist of them all," but in Cuba the marvel was that he went as far as he did. After securing passage home on a hospital ship, he wrote about and painted the ordinary soldier (plate 46). His text and

illustrations were mainly about the wounded not the valiant, the muck not the glory.

Following the war, Remington was a star once more, but he was depressed. To continue issuing his prints, the publisher R. H. Russell had to rely again on subjects from the 1897 book *Drawings* (plates 45, 48, 49, and 51).

Remington's fellow illustrator Howard Pyle told him of "a feeling that somehow you were not happy in your heart." This was true, for his daydreams of himself as a heroic cavalry officer like his gallant father were over. When *Collier's* sent him back to Cuba in 1899 to report on the army of occupation, he rallied his spirits to paint *A First-Class Fighting Man* (plate 50), but he refused to do a book of pictures glorifying the war. He was admittedly a prudent man, an artist and not a fighter. He weighed 295 pounds and drank heavily.

After an absence of four years, Remington entered *Missing* (plate 45) in the 1899 exhibition of the National Academy. The painting was not mentioned in critics' reviews, and that was the end of Remington's participation in Academy exhibitions. By 1900, however, no other American artist had equivalent name recognition. Remington was accumulating capital through earnings from his illustrations, and he was feeling a little better about himself.

He also fancied himself as an author. In this potboiling period in his art, he decided to challenge Owen Wister by writing a truer novel about the West than his former friend's conventional glorification of the Anglo cowboy at the expense of the real Tex-Mex cowboy, the Indian, and the cavalry. Remington picked as his protagonist a pre-reservation Indian successively named White Otter, the Bat, and Fire Eater, and he wrote about Indian life from his idea of the Indian standpoint. Naturally, he chose himself as illustrator (plates 52–60). The pictures were painted in color, although color was not used in many books in 1900.

After five years of delays, the novel *The Way of an Indian* was serialized in *Cosmopolitan* magazine starting in November 1905. The book was not published until 1906, when color was more common, but the reproductions of the illustrations were in black and white except for the frontispiece. The novel became one of the *High Spots of American Literature* in Merle Johnson's book, but it was not as commercially successful as Wister's book *The Virginian*.

44.

The Charge of the Rough Riders

1899. Despite Remington's unwillingness to depict the Cuban war, he agreed to do *The Charge* to illustrate Roosevelt's 1899 article "The Rough Riders." Roosevelt called it a "good picture," though "individual faces," including his, were not identifiable.
[Frederic Remington Art Museum]

45.

Missing, a.k.a. The Captive

1899. *Missing* was painted in color for the 1899 exhibition of the National Academy of Design, where it attracted little attention. The picture was reproduced in black and white, perhaps because the publisher considered Remington's color sense to be deficient.
[Frederic Remington Art Museum]

46.

**Scream of the Shrapnel,
a.k.a. Before the
Warning Scream of the
Shrapnel**

1899. "Our soldiers of San
Juan were under fire, subject
to wounds and death before
they had a chance to know
where the enemy was. They
flattened themselves before
the warning scream of the
shrapnel, but that is the
proper thing to do."
—*Harper's Monthly,* 11/1898,
page 965
[Authors' collection,
tear sheet]

QUESTIONABLE COMPANIONSHIP.—DRAWN BY FREDERIC REMINGTON.—[SEE PAGE 627.]

47.

Questionable Companionship

1899. "As the Indian wheels beside you, his cold eye takes in every article of apparel, arms, and ornament. He is poor, lawless, and covetous. Some add he is treacherous. There are narrow places ahead for single-file riding."—*Harper's Weekly,* 8/9/1890, page 627 [Authors' collection, tear sheet].

48.

Forsythe's Fight on the Republican River, 1868, a.k.a. *The Charge of Roman Nose*

1899. On June 16, 1886, during his first trip west as an illustrator, Remington found General George Forsyth [*sic*] to be "one of those men who you can bet would fight quick and long. I like him on first meeting more than any man I ever met. I'll immortelize him some day." [Frederic Remington Art Museum]

49.
Half-Breed Horse Thieves
of the Northwest

1899. Remington was concerned about the place of "half-breed" men in the West. He thought they might have become a separate ethnic group, but he never mentioned the biracial daughters of white employees of the fur companies and Indian women.
[The Thomas Gilcrease Institute of American History and Art]

50.
A First-Class
Fighting Man

1899. According to Remington, "The thing about our regulars which struck the foreign attachés who came here to observe our Spanish war was his unbuttoned negligence in dress. This is because he is an American and that is the national character."—*Collier's Weekly*, 3/25/1899, page 12
[Authors' collection, tear sheet]

FREDERIC REMINGTON'S

A
Fine
Artist's
Proof

ON HEAVY PLATE PAPER, MEASURING 16 x 22 inches SUITABLE FOR FRAMING, SENT ON RECEIPT OF

50 cents

ADDRESS

Art Department
COLLIER'S WEEKLY
521 West 13th Street
NEW YORK CITY

"A FIRST-CLASS FIGHTING MAN"

51.
A Crow Scout

1900. The traditional pictorial treatment of the equine gallop had been the hobbyhorse with legs extended to front and rear. Remington's sympathizers said he was the first to give character to the horse in art and the first to draw horses with all hooves off the ground in the tuck position.
[Amon Carter Museum]

52.
O Gray Wolf of My Clan, Shall We Have Fortune?

1906 [painted in 1900]. Red Arrow asked, "Tell me, pretty wolf, shall White Otter's and my scalps be danced by the Absaroke?"—*The Way of an Indian,* page 43. Roosevelt wrote Remington, "It may be that no white man ever understood an Indian, but you convey the impression of understanding him!"
[Richard Myers collection]

53.
Pretty Mother of the Night—White Otter Is No Longer a Boy

1906 [1900]. White Otter spoke: "Pretty Mother of the Night—White Otter is no longer a boy." Then to his pony: "You shall never carry any man but White Otter, and that only in war."—*The Way of an Indian,* page 56. The royalties earned in the first year following publication of *The Way of an Indian* were fifty dollars.

[Richard Myers collection]

54.

The Interpreter Waved at the Naked Youth, Sitting There on His War-Pony, a.k.a. The Interpreter Pointed to White Otter on His War-Pony

1906 [1900]. The boy White Otter had been superseded by the man, the Bat. At last it became time for the Bat to go into the traders' circle. Ah, a rifle! That was what the Bat wanted. The interpreter waved, "Go away." Indians sprang between them.—*The Way of an Indian,* page 75 [Richard Myers collection]

55.

I Will Tell the White Man How He Can Have His Ponies Back, a.k.a. White Otter Defies the White Man

1906 [1900]. The young Indian gained the center of the lodge. "I will tell the white man how he can have his ponies back. He can hand over to me the bright new gun which lies by his side." McIntish raised the rifle, then threw it in front of the Bat. —*The Way of an Indian,* page 93 [Richard Myers collection]

56.

Nothing but Cheerful Looks Followed the Bat, a.k.a. _Admiring Eyes Followed White Otter_

1906 [1900]. As the Bat passed women, he began to think of taking one. He stepped inside and saw a young squaw beading. There are no preliminaries when a savage warrior concludes to act. The abruptness of the Bat's love-making left room for few words.—_The Way of an Indian,_ page 108 [Richard Myers collection]

57.

The Ceremony of the Fastest Horse, a.k.a. _Over the Prairie Fled White Otter with His Stolen Bride_

1906 [1900]. The Bat had wandered [back] to the Fort. Looking up, he saw she was on the roof. She slid down on a lariat. They got to the pony-herds where the Bat mounted his new woman on one. They were married by the Ceremony of the Fastest Horse.—_The Way of an Indian,_ page 115 [Richard Myers collection]

58.

The Fire Eater Raised His Arms to the Thunder Bird,* a.k.a. *The Fire Eater Raised His Arms Heavenward

1906 [1900]. The Thunder Bird had spoken to Fire Eater: "Go to the Absaroke—your gun wants to talk to them." In response to Fire Eater, they had charged the stockade. The medicine was bad. Standing on the bank, he raised his arms to the Thunder Bird.—*The Way of an Indian,* page 161 [Richard Myers collection]

59.

The Rushing Red Lodges Passed through the Line of the Blue Soldiers, a.k.a. White Otter Led the Charge

1906 [1900]. Sitting Bull, Crazy Horse, and the strong men talked. A mounted rider cut by, shrieking, "The pony-soldiers are coming over the hills!" The rushing Red Lodges passed through the line, striking with their axes.—*The Way of an Indian,* page 210 [Richard Myers collection]

60.

He Made His Magazine Gun Blaze until Empty, a.k.a. *White Otter at Bay Emptied His Magazine Gun*

1906 [1900]. When the old warrior heard a rifle shot, he snatched his precious boy and ran out. Putting the boy down, he made his gun blaze until empty. He knew the shadow had gone. The Fire Eater wanted to go where Cheyennes of his youth were at peace.—*The Way of an Indian*, page 252 [Richard Myers collection]

Changing Techniques

A Critical Moment
(plate 79, detail)

In the spring of 1899, *Harper's* unexpectedly found itself in deep financial trouble. One of the magazine's first moves was to fire Remington and retain cheaper illustrators. The loyal Remington was enraged, but he soon caught on with *Collier's Weekly* magazine, which paid him more, promoted his work more, and convinced him that he was appreciated and needed. He promptly recovered from any trace of his war-born depression.

Collier's was already carrying advertisements by the Colonial Press for the sale of prints of Admiral George Dewey, the hero of Manila Bay. In August 1899, *Collier's* art department offered its own print, Remington's *A First-Class Fighting Man* (plate 50), for fifty cents. The response was weak so no other Remington print was produced until

April 1901, when *A Monte Game at the Southern Ute Agency* (plate 61) was tested. Five more black-and-white prints were produced in three months, and then there was another pause.

It is impossible to know exactly how many prints were issued at this time. *Collier's* advertised, "Send $1 and we will send a proof" of a Gibson girl drawing "or of any other picture you may select," including Remingtons. Presumably a subscriber could order any double- or single-page Remington illustration and *Collier's* would run off a reproduction of it for a dollar.

The prints of this period were in both black and white and color. *The Cowpuncher* (plate 64) was painted in color, run in black and white in the magazine, issued as a black-and-white print, and later reproduced in color as a print. To enhance the publication of *The Cowpuncher,* the art editor sent a wire to Owen Wister: "Can you mail us tomorrow quatrain to go with spirited drawing by Remington, mounted cowboy about to throw lariat, wire answer." Wister's poem characterized the confident cowpuncher as pitiable rather than cocky, but Remington loved it. "Sort of put the d- - - - - public under the skin," he enthused.

In December 1901, *Collier's* presented *Caught in the Circle* (plate 75) in full color. That was the breakthrough for color in the magazine and for volume sales of *Collier's* prints. The picture was a classic pyramidal composition focusing on action at the apex. While earlier Indian surrounds had been canvases filled with detail, *Caught in the Circle* was greatly simplified. Its corners contained just enough particulars to support the employment of asymmetrical motion. Novelist Frank Norris was so inspired that he wrote a story enlarging on the fictitious incident.

R. H. Russell published even more color prints. He made eight Remington pastels into the vivid portfolio *A Bunch of Buckskins* (plates 67–74). These reproductions are among the few Remington prints that have significant monetary value at present. One edition of

the portfolio was auctioned for $11,000 in 1988.

The pastels were included in Remington's first solo gallery exhibition as a serious painter in December 1901. The art critics agreed, "We are not claiming Mr. Remington displays subtle feeling for color but the years have brought ease of expression with a clearer sense of composition." He was getting better at what he had been doing for fifteen years. He was not yet doing it well enough, however, to satisfy the pundits whose opinions he valued most.

Wister wrote the introduction for *A Bunch of Buckskins.* He acknowledged that Remington "creates a personality" in each drawing, to such an extent that the writer actively disliked *Old Ramon* (plate 70). Remington's reply was sad: "October 4 & I am 40 years old to day. Its a down hill pull from here."

The following year Scribner's produced a boxed set of four Remington color prints, *Western Types* (plates 80–83). They too have value today.

The first of the four prints for Smith & Wesson, *The Last Stand* (plate 76), in black and white, was an example of Remington's recycled titles. *Twenty-five to One* (plate 33) was also known as *The Last Stand,* and *Caught in the Circle* expressly depicted a last stand. A print that has had three or four names over the years may be a poorer composition, needing the strength of a colorful appellation, although several names for one print and several prints bearing the same name cause considerable confusion in identification. On the other hand, classic prints such as *An Evening on a Canadian Lake* (plate 100) and *With the Eye of the Mind* (plate 130) generally have only one title.

Changes in titles over the years can be amusing. After Remington died, *Goose Shooting* (plate 8) became *Pheasant Shooting,* although the birds were clearly Canada geese. *A Cheyenne Buck* (plate 67) switched tribes to become *A Black-foot Brave. With the Wolfhounds* (plate 77) was also known as *Coursing Wolves with Greyhounds,* an improvement because Remington knew that cavalry officers such as Powhatan Clarke had greyhounds, not wolfhounds.

61.
A Monte Game at the Southern Ute Agency, a.k.a. Mexican Monte

1901. Remington explained that "as the Indians gather about the trader's store, one of them spreads his blanket on the sand and begins to deal monte. If the military bodies were to [try to] stop one of these things by force they could not do it."
—*Collier's Weekly,* 4/20/1901, page 12. In 1900, no Remington painting in *Collier's* had been issued as a print. In 1901, eight were reproduced. [Frederic Remington Art Museum]

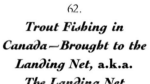

62.
Trout Fishing in Canada—Brought to the Landing Net, a.k.a. The Landing Net

1901. The *Collier's* art director wrote Remington, "Your trout fishing picture is bully. You're doing better work all the time. I want more—more!" Remington was a regular visitor to Canada. Fishing was a favorite sport, though he claimed "others fish, I sketch." [Amon Carter Museum]

63.

Killing a Cattle Thief, a.k.a. *At Last*

1901. Remington described the scene: "A party of cowboys have run down and surrounded a grizzly bear, the most cunning and wary of cattle thieves."—*Collier's Weekly,* 9/7/1901, page 12 [The Library of Congress]

64.

The Cowpuncher, a.k.a. *No More He Rides*

1901. Owen Wister's garbled quatrain was, "No more he rides, yon waif of night; / His was the song the eagle sings; / Strong as the eagle's his delight, / For like his rope, his heart had wings." "That verse was a corkarina," Remington applauded. [Richard F. Brush Art Gallery, St. Lawrence University]

65.
A Post Office in the "Cow Country," a.k.a. Latest News

1901. The art editor at *Collier's* cheered Remington on. He wrote, "The pictures which Fred Remington hath wrought / Are with suave and finished beauty fraught. Keep on sending 'em." Pictures like the mailbox in the desert became Western stereotypes. [The Library of Congress]

66.
Calling the Moose, a.k.a. Calling to the Moose, a.k.a. Calling to Death

1901. Remington was fired by *Harper's* because of the magazine's financial difficulties. *Collier's* paid better and reproduced as many as two paintings a month as covers, frontispieces, or double pages, then issued the most popular of them again as prints. [The R. W. Norton Art Gallery]

67.

A Cheyenne Buck, a.k.a.
An Indian Brave, a.k.a.
A Black-foot Brave

1901. The eight pastels for
R. H. Russell were a burst of
savage color. Remington
thought they were incendiary.
He said, "When the shoppies
put them in their windows,
passing fire engines will
stop & hook into the
adjoining hydrant."
[Whitney Gallery of
Western Art, Buffalo Bill
Historical Center]

68.

A Sioux Chief, a.k.a.
A War Chief

1901. Remington was so
pleased by Owen Wister's
introduction, he said he
blushed: "When I read it Ex-
tract of Vermillion would
make a blue mark on my
face. I have to put on my
smoked glasses." The
publisher told Wister, "I
enclose 25 dollars."
[Whitney Gallery of
Western Art, Buffalo Bill
Historical Center]

69.

A Breed, a.k.a.
An Indian Scout, a.k.a.
A North-west Half Breed

1901. The publisher had sent
Wister proofs without identi-
fying the subjects. He had to
correct Wister, "You have described the Mexican border-
er, known as 'Old Ramon,'
as the 'half-breed.' The
Half Breed is the man without
a hat, with a spotted horse."
[Whitney Gallery of
Western Art, Buffalo Bill
Historical Center]

70.

Old Ramon, also with A
Mexican Half-Breed
added

1901. Wister admitted, "Old
Ramon may have scouted for
the military," but he insisted
Ramon's parents had
spawned double evil and
worthlessness, evidenced by a
haymaker hat, contemptible
saddle blanket, splintered
rifle stock, and stolen horse.
[Whitney Gallery of
Western Art, Buffalo Bill
Historical Center]

71.
A Cavalry Officer
1901. The figure is reminiscent of General Custer. This is the cavalry officer of the Plains Indian wars, not the 1898 Spanish-American War. His outfit reflects the disregard for the military dress code by officers in the West.
[Whitney Gallery of Western Art, Buffalo Bill Historical Center]

72.
An Army Packer, a.k.a. *A Regular*
1901. Remington sent Roosevelt a presentation copy of *A Bunch of Buckskins.* The acknowledgment, "I appreciate the pictures as I always do everything of yours," came from the president of the United States. McKinley had been murdered in Buffalo.
[Whitney Gallery of Western Art, Buffalo Bill Historical Center]

73.

An Arizona Cowboy

1901. Remington told a patron in 1896, "It is fortunate you know the greatest handler of pastels—the undersigned. I tried my first shot at my old mare and Columbus when he discovered America or the boy when he discovers the moon were not half so tickled."
[Whitney Gallery of Western Art, Buffalo Bill Historical Center]

74.

A Trapper, a.k.a. An Old Time Trapper

1901. This is a trapper spruced up for the portrait. Normally, Remington would have drawn him as "the free trapper, weather-beaten and tough, galloping into camp with his fine horse and his splendid trappings, hungry for a holiday," to quote Wister.
[Whitney Gallery of Western Art, Buffalo Bill Historical Center]

75.

Caught in the Circle

1901. The magazine legend was, "The last stand of troopers and a scout overtaken by hostile Indians."—*Collier's Weekly,* 12/7/1901, page 20. A comparable subject in 1889 was *The Last Lull in the Fight,* where there were "grotesque horse carcasses and a litter of arrows, bandages, and blood." [Authors' collection]

76.

The Last Stand

1902. Smith & Wesson advertised, "For smoking room or
den we have published a limited number of copies on
heavy plate paper we will
send prepaid for ten cents in
silver, together with small
reproductions of pictures
which have appeared
previously."
[Smith & Wesson]

77.

**With the Wolfhounds,
a.k.a. Coursing Wolves
with Greyhounds**

1902. In 1902, Remington
believed he was not being
sufficiently selective in com-
missions he accepted from
magazines. Yet he sold reproduction rights to companies
like Smith & Wesson.
Advertising paid more
than magazines did.
[Smith & Wesson]

78.

Hands Off

1902. This print appeared as
a Smith & Wesson advertisement in *Scribner's* and *The
Cosmopolitan* magazines in
August 1902: "A Smith &
Wesson inspires confidence
to the hand that holds it,
and respect from the
unwelcome visitor."
[Smith & Wesson]

79.

A Critical Moment

1902. The least of the four
Smith & Wesson prints, *A
Critical Moment* was issued in
small numbers for ten cents.
By the 1940s the print was
described as scarce and
was offered at twenty-five
dollars. The current price
would be in excess of
three hundred dollars.
[Smith & Wesson]

80.
The Cow-boy
1902. Remington wrote, "The cow-boy is trying to get mountain-bred ponies to go where he wants. Knowing the 'Irish pig' of their nature, he has to be insistent; all of which represents a type of 'pony footing' easier to delineate than to perform."
—*Scribner's Magazine,* 10/1902, page 409
[The Rockwell Museum]

81.
The Cossack Post (Cavalryman)

1902. "A picket of three men is called a 'Cossack post,' and the moonlight uncovers a Cavalryman on the Northern plains in the almost fierce and certainly definite light of a country which has 'no atmosphere,' as painters phrase it."—*Scribner's Magazine,* 10/1902, page 411
[The Rockwell Museum]

82.
The Scout

1902. "The Scout. Too well known to need particular comment, he was the white hunter who had gone to the wild countries and was employed by our troops for light-horse work in a country and among a people unknown to the Army." —*Scribner's Magazine,* 10/1902, page 413
[The Rockwell Museum]

83.
The Half-Breed

1902. "A relic of the fur company days—the descendant of white employees and Indian squaws. They led a nomad existence on the plains and bid fair to become a separate people. They still exist [in 1902], though robbed of characteristic traits."—*Scribner's Magazine,* 10/1902, page 415

[The Rockwell Museum]

The Superstar

The Bell Mare
(plate 93, detail)

By 1902, Remington was established as the best-known American artist. As his artistic power grew, though, his vaunted physical strength was dissipating. He described himself as "bald headed and one legged and the curves are more easily followed."

He was still specializing in frontiersmen, cavalry, cowboys, and Indians of the Old West, but privately he was disappointed in what he was finding on his infrequent sketching trips to the mountain states to refresh his images. He threatened "never to come West again—it is all brick buildings—derby hats and blue overhauls—it spoils my early illusions." He deprecated the Utes in Colorado as "to[o] far on the road to civilization to be distinctive." In New Mexico he "did not like pueblas—

blue gingham breeches did for me—too tame."

Despite Remington's popularity, *Collier's* bought reproduction rights to only a few of his paintings in 1902 and then just to illustrate stories in the magazine. No print of his was issued by *Collier's* that year.

Late in 1903, *Collier's* decided to feature Remington's Western paintings in the magazine again to boost further a circulation that was close to tripling. By this time, Remington had made up his mind to concentrate on fine art and avoid any magazine work that might be construed as illustration. He resisted the offer by *Collier's,* causing art editor George Wharton Edwards to plead with him, "I want some DRAWINGS now— wine hell can't I have some of Ewers?" ("Ewers" meant "yours.")

Remington was soon seduced by the money, five hundred dollars a month at the start and then a thousand, at a time when five hundred dollars was a good year's pay for a teacher or minister. Also, the agreement stipulated that he could choose his own subjects for reproduction in color so he would not be interpreting another person's text. Edwards told him, "Your art is young, the best is yet to be, / What is to come not even they [the critics] foresee."

The schedule called for a full-color double-page Western picture or a cover for each fiction issue of the magazine, the one that appeared the second week of every month. Tens of thousands of *Collier's* subscribers waited impatiently for their fiction issues to come in the mail. Hundreds of them bought the prints *Collier's* offered.

Remington responded with dedication. He used to say that some of his "best things" were done in an hour. Now he employed a model rather than working "chic," and a painting could take a week. He also searched for authentic detail. In *His First Lesson* (plate 84), for example, the colt standing sideways has his right rear leg tied up to inhibit kicking during training.

Remington had been friends with other leading illustrators such as Charles Dana Gibson and Edward Kemble since he started in art. There was no competition among them. Each had his own specialty. Gibson drew girls and Kemble drew blacks, while Remington painted the West. He socialized with other painters, including Winslow Homer, a leading fine artist (fig. 6).

By 1903, his companions were The Ten American Painters, the Impressionists who were refining an American version of what had originally been a French technique. They were at the crest of American fine art then, as their works remain now, and Remington painted alongside them. He also learned from Monet's paintings, which were on exhibition in New York City. His brushwork became brisker, black was on his palette less frequently, and pure colors alternated on the canvas. He considered himself to be competitive with The Ten and at least as talented.

Influenced by the art he saw around him, Remington also became preoccupied with catching night effects on canvas. Critics noted the change "where a painter took the place of the illustrator's blaring reds and yellows." On the other hand, *Collier's* still resisted any departure from glaring high noon as the setting for its pictures and did not reproduce a true nocturne as a print until *A Night Attack on a Government Wagon Train* (plate 91) in June 1904.

For his first paintings to be run as a series in *Collier's,* Remington decided to offer his fans a history lesson to tie in with the 1904 Louisiana Purchase Exposition. The subjects of his essay in paint ranged from pioneers (plate 87) to traders (plate 88), trappers (plate 89), Indian resistance, soldiers, ranchers, cattle drives, stagecoaches, and finally the end of the Old West era (plate 97). Today these paintings look like stills from a Western movie. They set the style, seemingly forever, for popular Western art and fiction as well as the cinema.

In addition to color, Remington's key technical commitment at this point was to composition. He explained that "big art is the process of elimination. Cut down and out—do your hardest work outside the picture, and let your audience take away something to think about." His trick was to stop the action before the conclusion, as he did in *The Emigrants* (plate 90).

His subject matter was restricted to the West. He sailed the St. Lawrence River on an excursion boat and "saw nothing worth while. I guess I am getting to be an old swat—I can't see anything that didn't happen twenty years ago." Even his central figures were only semirealized. Backgrounds were loose and unspecific. Daylight colors were becoming muted. The models he chose could be surprises. He wrote, "Have been painting Jersey cows all day—getting ready to do Texas Longhorns because they have the same color" (plate 96).

After Remington applied all of his artifices to create a painting that suited him, the *Collier's* editors took over. In 1901, they had written on the print they sent him of *A Monte Game,* "compliments of Collier's Weekly." They wanted to show him how precisely the reproduction conformed to his painting. Now, however, not only did they insist on action in broad daylight, they wanted the figures drawn large so the space allotted in the magazine would be filled with actors. Without regard for the niceties of the artist's compositional design, they cropped the photographs of the pictures, sometimes on all four sides, to gain a tighter focus.

Remington's penchant was to sign his pictures in the lower right corner. Frequently the signature was removed by the editors in the course of their cropping for the magazine. In the early days they added back into the uncropped area a signature lifted from the photograph of another painting. Later they left the pictures in the magazine unsigned. Their excuse was that no one could fail to recognize the hand of this artist.

In the production of prints, they duplicated the way the pictures were cropped in the magazine. Occasionally the prints were cropped further to fit a smaller space. Enlargements were usually made by increasing the paper size, not expanding the image. Whenever the print was scaled up or down in dimension, *Collier's* generally filed for a new copyright.

Thus, *Collier's* subscribers had no idea that some of Remington's pictures published in the magazine had been cut down in size. They did not know that among the pictures they enjoyed were what today would be recognized as details of paintings. In effect, they approved of the cropping by buying so many prints by Remington and other *Collier's* illustrators that the art department could not handle the volume. A separate proof department was organized in 1904.

Remington paid no attention to the prints. He was with *Collier's* for the money. Apart from that, his abiding interest was fine art. At his gallery shows, the paintings whose publication rights he had sold to the magazine were exhibited in their original dimensions. Only the photographic images had been cut down.

Figure 6. Playing cards with Winslow Homer. [Authors' collection]

84.

His First Lesson

1903. This was the first of the new series reproduced by *Collier's* in full color. The print was re-copyrighted in 1908 because of severe cropping left, bottom, and right to emphasize action. A new signature and the date were added. Remington never objected.

[Authors' collection]

The Fight for the Water Hole

1903. The subject kindled enthusiasm in Remington fans, "boys between 12 and 70." The Abilene chief of police asked Remington which defender had described the scene to him because the chief claimed to remember the site of what was really a make-believe fight.
[Authors' collection]

86.

The Creek Indian, a.k.a. The Indian Head

1903. When Remington's friends saw a picture of a social function at the White House, they knew he had either been there or had turned the invitation down President Theodore Roosevelt was a Remington fan with a print of *The Creek Indian* in his Oyster Bay home.
[The Library of Congress]

87.
The Pioneers

1904. According to the magazine caption, "This is the first of a series of 12 paintings by Frederic Remington illustrative of the Louisiana Purchase Period." The pictorial essay was tied in with the Louisiana Purchase Exposition in St. Louis.—*Collier's Weekly,* 2/13/1904, page 18 [Richard F. Brush Art Gallery, St. Lawrence University]

88.
The Santa Fe Trade

1904. This is "a Wagon Train on its journey from Missouri through the Louisiana Territory toward Santa Fe and Chihuahua." As the population of whites increased in the new lands, settlers were supplied with goods by wagons like these.—*Collier's Weekly,* 3/12/1904, page 16 [Richard F. Brush Art Gallery, St. Lawrence University]

89.
The Gathering of the Trappers, a.k.a. Trappers Going to the Rendezvous, a.k.a. The Rendezvous
1904. In this third of the Louisiana Purchase series, Remington was again painting history. The annual rendezvous of the mountain men to sell their skins to the fur companies and to celebrate had begun in 1825. By the 1840s it was over.
[Authors' collection]

90.

The Emigrants

1904. As the trappers' rendezvous ended, thousands of emigrants were westward-bound in wagons, despite hardships and loss of lives from accident and disease. The threat of Indian attacks was not as great as Remington led his public to expect.
[National Cowboy Hall of Fame and Western Heritage Center]

91.

A Night Attack on a Government Wagon Train

1904. In 1899, Remington was concerned about his inability to capture colors. The key to improvement came from an exhibition of California nocturnes that led him to try mastering "the nuances of the moon's witchery in all her moods."
[Frederic Remington Art Museum]

92.

Drifting before the Storm
1904. "In [the] early days," Remington wrote, "storms drove the cattle irresistibly before them. The cowboys, not able to handle the frightened and half-frozen animals, were forced to drift with them, often for a hundred miles, living as best they could."—*Collier's Weekly,* 7/9/1904, page 14 [Frederic Remington Art Museum]

93.

***The Bell Mare*, a.k.a.**
In the Enemy's Country

1904. Charley Russell saw this
serene print after Remington
died. The title had been
changed to *In the Enemy's
Country.* Russell groused that
if the pack train was in hostile territory, "then why the
hell did he leave that God
damn bell on the lead
horse's neck?"
[Authors' collection]

94.

***The Stampede*, a.k.a.**
A Change of Ownership

1904. Remington explained,
"It was a frequent occurrence
in the pioneer days for Indians to rush a corral or the
camp of an emigrant train,
shouting and waving their
blankets, frightening the
horses, who would be cap-
tured ultimately by the
Indians."—*Collier's Weekly,*
9/10/1904, page 14
[Richard F. Brush Art Gallery, St. Lawrence University]

95.

Pony Tracks in the Buffalo Trail

1904. An Indian ruse has failed to work. "A scouting party in advance of a column of soldiers [is] picking up Indians signs," Remington observed. "They have found pony tracks among those of the buffalo, and the scouts are trying to pick up the trail."—*Collier's Weekly,* 10/8/1904, page 16 [Authors' collection]

96.

Trailing Texas Cattle

1904. According to the magazine caption, "Thirty years ago, herds of 'longhorn' Texas cattle were driven from the lower country to ship East as beef or to stock northern ranges. This shows a drive coming on in the flood of a gorgeous Western sunset."—*Collier's Weekly,* 11/12/1904, page 16 [Authors' collection]

97.

The End of the Day

1904. *The End of the Day*
symbolized the end of Remington's Old West. Frontiersmen were long gone. Indians
were subdued. The army had
no role in the West. Cowboys
were animal "farmers." Now
Remington's subjects for
paintings could come only
from his memory.
[Frederic Remington
Art Museum]

98.

***An Argument with the
Town Marshal***

1905. Western towns elected
lawmen like Pat Garrett,
Wild Bill Hickok, Bat
Masterson, and Wyatt Earp.
Marshals worked late on Sat-
urday nights, when a cowboy
might shoot up the town.
This scene is old Front
Street, Dodge City, Kansas.
[National Cowboy Hall
of Fame and Western
Heritage Center]

Blending Art into Illustration

A Halt in the Wilderness
(plate 106, detail)

In March 1905, the original Remington paintings for the previous year's *Collier's* series were exhibited in New York City. The prominent art critic Royal Cortissoz wrote, "So full of life they are, and oh! so rippingly painted, making something beautiful no one else could make."

In contrast, fellow artist Samuel Isham on behalf of the National Academicians was disparaging: "The subject is more to him than the purely artistic qualities." Action was Remington's special subject, as Cortissoz had recognized. Nevertheless, if Remington was to satisfy his exacting peers he would have to relinquish his strongest suit.

Oddly enough, he was prepared to do just that. His friends The Ten American Painters also advocated symbolism over realism. They were now Remington's most

powerful influences and they abhorred storytelling with paint. His history of having been an illustrator was not by itself a black mark with them. Hassam, Metcalf, Twachtman, and Weir had all been illustrators, if not as successful as Remington was. They had abandoned narrative painting and they pressed him to do the same.

Even after Remington was ready to acquiesce to the prevailing artistic standard, however, the roadblock to his acceptance as a symbolist remained his obligation to *Collier's.* The magazine was still totally opposed to blandness or passivity in the art it bought from him. On the other hand, *Collier's* was the source of his most publicized tribute. The entire March 18, 1905, issue of the magazine was labeled the Remington Number, reproducing his paintings and sculpture along with articles about him and one by him. In the face of such dedication, Remington could not be angry with his employer, however obdurate the editors were.

The cover of the Remington Number was a pastel of a mounted, middle-aged, decrepit yet appealing Indian, mouth open in greeting and waving his right hand with its abbreviated ring finger (plate 99).

The featured painting was the tranquil centerfold, the highly simplified nocturne *An Evening on a Canadian Lake* (plate 100), which continues to be a most popular work in modern exhibitions. The composition is deceptively open. The background is divided in half by the diagonal line from upper left to lower right. The break in the treeline at top left is repeated by the reflection of the bow of the canoe. The background colors are dark and rich, giving added prominence to the canoeists.

The introduction by Owen Wister was reprinted from an earlier Remington book. By 1905, the novelist and the artist pictured here in front of the mantel (fig. 7) were no longer close friends. They thought they had passed the point where they needed each other to enhance their professional efforts.

The lead article was by Richard Harding Davis's brother Charles, suggesting that at Remington's birth, "the good fairies gathered to bestow many talents." There was another article on Remington's bronze sculpture, and then there were "A Few Words" from the maestro himself: "Evening overtook me one night in Montana, and I made the camp-fire of an old wagon freighter. I was nineteen. I knew the railroad was coming. I knew the derby hats, the smoking chimneys, the cord-binder [for sheaves of grain], and the thirty-day note were upon us. I saw the living, breathing end of three American centuries of smoke and dust and sweat, and I now see quite another thing where it all took place, but it does not appeal to me."

The whole *Collier's* issue was, in effect, a Remington sales catalog. The paintings were available at Noe Art Galleries on Fifth Avenue. The bronze statuettes were offered at Tiffany's. Remington's annual earnings were now estimated at $50,000.

The magazine's appetite for daylight action had not abated, but Remington's popularity was so immense that he was finally able to persuade *Collier's* to publish his nocturnes regularly. The editors had been withholding *A Reconnaissance* (plate 101) since 1902, despite favorable reviews when the painting was exhibited in 1903. In 1905, five of the next six prints issued by the magazine, including *A Reconnaissance,* were night scenes. However, only *Coming to the Call* (plate 105) sold in a quantity that satisfied *Collier's.* In 1984, the original painting of *Coming to the Call* was purchased at public auction for $500,000.

As late as 1970, the fashion among some sophisticated museum curators was to be sarcastic about Remington and his work. The caption for *A Reconnaissance* was criticized as an inaccurate description. It observed that the cavalry officer was spying safely from behind the tree line, whereas the critics insisted that the officer was really vulnerable out in the open while the Indians were protected by the forest.

Figure 7. The artist in front of the mantel. [Frederic Remington Art Museum]

99.
The Chieftain, a.k.a. Indian on Horse

1905. Owen Wister wrote in *Collier's* Remington Number, "Remington is not merely an artist; he is a national treasure. I should like to hear him receive his degree in these words: 'Frederic Remington, Draughtsman, Historian, Poet.'"
[Frederic Remington Art Museum]

100.
An Evening on a Canadian Lake

1905. A photograph in the magazine posed Remington as an Easterner with Indian artifacts behind him. There was also an ad by the Acme Drawing School, citing Remington to show what could be accomplished by correspondence, although Remington had no connection with the school.
[Authors' collection]

101.

**A Reconnaissance, a.k.a.
A Reconnaissance in the
Moonlight**

1905. According to the magazine caption, "A cavalry officer with his white scout [is] viewing hostile Indian country by moonlight from the protection of trees." The nocturne, which was dated 1902, was withheld by *Collier's* until 1905.—*Collier's Weekly,* 4/8/1905, page 18
[Frederic Remington
Art Museum]

102.

**An Old Story in a
New Way**

1905. Although *Collier's* wanted only "violent Western action in daylight or classic Indian symbolism," Remington persuaded the editor to feature *An Old Story in a New Way.* By 1905 the obese artist was using a naphtha "put-put" at his summer home in place of a Rushton canoe.
[The Rockwell Museum]

103.
The Buffalo Runners

1905. There is a platemaker's error in some of these buffalo prints. Yellow dust rises to fill the space under the Indian's arm and spear instead of remaining at the horizon. Remington did few scenes of Indians killing buffalo compared to Charley Russell, who painted tens of them.
[Authors' collection]

104.
An Early Start for Market, a.k.a. On the Road to Market

1905. After the Louisiana Purchase series, the paintings reproduced as prints in 1905 favored a darker palette in continuing the historical theme of a period Remington knew. *An Early Start for Market* was a new, peaceful variation on old fantasies.
[Frederic Remington Art Museum]

105.
Coming to the Call

1905. *Coming to the Call* was
the continuation of the 1901
Calling the Moose. Although
the painting is abstracted,
simplified in color, and not
Western, it was one of Remington's most popular prints.
The surface is like
inlays of old leather in
rich hues.
[Authors' collection]

106.
A Halt in the Wilderness

1905. This was the end of
Remington's joy ride with
Collier's. The art editor re-
signed and thereafter Reming-
ton did not stay with his
proven formula of cowboys,
Indians, and cavalrymen.
He began searching for
what he saw as "purely
artistic qualities."
[Frederic Remington
Art Museum]

Going Wrong

Radisson and Groseilliers
(plate 109, detail)

Remington started the latter part of 1905 heading in the wrong direction as far as his relationship with *Collier's* was concerned. His employer, Bobbie Collier, was quickly unhappy.

Art editor George Wharton Edwards had resigned under pressure, and with him went the friendly restraints that had kept Remington on a productive high-keyed track for the magazine. Left to his own, the artist conceived a ten-part *The Great American Explorers* series. His intent was to satisfy *Collier's* by telling thrilling tales as he had in the popular Louisiana Purchase paintings (plates 87–97). At the same time he would please the critics by creating beauty, as in the "Hiawatha" illustrations (plates 9–12). In "Hiawatha" he had succeeded despite admittedly superficial research, and he

confidently expected the same result here.

When the paintings of *The Explorers* series were finished, however, *Collier's* viewed them as if they were routine illustrations for grade-school texts rather than exciting art meant for the readers of a mass publication. In addition, Remington's captions in the magazine were duller than the pictures, a poor stimulus for the imagination of the artist's public. In a bitter betrayal of its own artist, *Collier's* took the extreme step of publishing abusive letters from subscribers. Because Remington had controlled the choice and execution of the subjects, he had no one to blame but himself.

Surprisingly, eight of the ten paintings were issued as prints (plates 107–114). Only *Radisson and Groseilliers* (plate 109) and *Zebulon Pike Entering Santa Fe* (plate 113) were received at all well.

In February 1906, Noe Art Galleries exhibited the originals of the ill-advised *The Great American Explorers* paintings and their more successful follow-up *The Unknown Explorers* (plate 115). Only *Radisson* sold.

Despite Remington's emphasis on a search for beauty at the expense of realism in order to please the critics, the reviews were restrained, too. *The Explorers* were judged to be no more than illustrations of stories. The paintings were not fine art, which was said to call for complete denial of the subject in favor of symbol-ism and sublimity. His colors were considered to be off, too. Remington acknowledged, "For ten years I've been trying to get color in my things and I still don't get it. I know fine color when I see it but it's maddening."

In the end, Remington had not satisfied the magazine, the public, the critics, or himself in *The Great American Explorers* series. His usefulness to the magazine was diminished. The whole year had been a setback.

From today's standpoint, the contretemps over *The Explorers* revealed that Remington's fans wanted to continue to be able to dream about exciting events in the romantic Old West rather than be saddled with long-forgotten historical subjects. On the other hand, while *The Explorers* paintings may have been off-putting in content, some of them were truly beautiful. The stylish depiction of *La Salle* (plate 110) is a prime example. In addition, *The Unknown Explorers* conveyed a real sense of danger that is missing in a bland reworking Remington did of the same subject in 1909. If not the magazine subscribers, at least the critics should have been satisfied.

Nevertheless, these are paintings Remington soon destroyed deliberately because they did not meet his peers' interpretation of the critical standards of the time. *Radisson and Groseilliers* escaped. For the rest of the series, only the prints remain.

107.

Hernando De Soto

1905. Even the caption was tame: "In 1539 De Soto led 600 men across our present Southern states to the Mississippi. The expedition constantly fought Indians but the greatest hardship was wading through miles of swamps."
—*Collier's Weekly*, 11/11/1905, page 8 [The Thomas Gilcrease Institute of American History and Art]

108.

The Expedition of Francisco Coronado

1905. The legend read, "Coronado was one of the earliest Spanish soldier explorers. With a large force he started from Mexico in 1540 and traveled across what is now New Mexico until he reached [the] present Kansas. Luckier than many, he returned to safety."—*Collier's Weekly,* 12/9/1905, page 8 [The Thomas Gilcrease Institute of American History and Art]

109.
Radisson and Groseilliers, a.k.a. Exploring the Lakes

1906. Remington's caption was, "Raddison a Frenchman together with Groseiller in 1659 voyaged west of Lake Superior and covered new territory near Hudson's Bay." The artist's research was so casual, he misspelled the names of both men.
—*Collier's Weekly,*
1/13/1906, page 8
[The Library of Congress]

110.
La Salle

1906. "Rene Robert Cavelier, Sieur de la Salle, was the explorer of the Mississippi," Remington wrote, "and there his gloomy life ended about 1682." The artist was concerned only with pictorial aspects, but at least his spelling of Cavelier was correct.
—*Collier's Weekly,*
2/10/1906, page 8
[The Thomas Gilcrease Institute of American History and Art]

111.

La Verendrye

1906. Remington told a play-
wright friend, "You want to
write about some place you
know—about a situation you
feel the heat of, and have
characters in it you love." He
did not follow his own advice
in *The Explorers* paintings.
[The Thomas Gilcrease
Institute of American
History and Art]

112.

Mackenzie

1906. This is the seventh in *The Explorers* series. Remington added only that, "Alexander Mackenzie, a chief trader of the Northwest Company, first crossed the Rocky Mountains in 1792 and penetrated to the Pacific Ocean."
—*Collier's Weekly,* 4/14/1906, page 8
[The Thomas Gilcrease Institute of American History and Art]

113.

Zebulon Pike Entering Santa Fe, a.k.a. A Spanish Escort

1906. Remington explained that Pike was an army officer sent on an 1807 expedition to fix the boundary with Mexico. The officer also discovered Pike's Peak. The picture shows the potentially hostile Spaniards escorting Pike and his men into Santa Fe. [Authors' collection]

114.

Jedediah Smith

1906. According to the caption, "This is the last picture of the series. It shows Smith making his way across the desert from Green River to the Spanish settlements at San Diego in 1826."

—*Collier's Weekly,*
7/14/1906, page 8.
Collier's, Remington, and the public were glad to see the series end.
[The Thomas Gilcrease Institute of American History and Art]

115.

The Unknown Explorers

1906. *Collier's* was printing
snide letters about Remington: "For the money he is
getting he ought to think up
something worth while, not
inane and meaningless pictures. He is not giving you
what you, and we, have
a right to demand—his
best work."

[Authors' collection]

The Painter Emerging Again

The Shadows at the Waterhole
(plate 123, detail)

In a discouraging end to 1906, Remington sidetracked himself again, this time with the misunderstood trilogy, *The Tragedy of the Trees* (plates 118–120). He hated the clear-cutting of the forests from an environmental standpoint, while the magazine assumed he was glorifying American industry. The public did not seem to care one way or the other.

Then, when it was almost too late to mend fences with *Collier's,* Remington began turning out a succession of the most fully realized Western paintings in the history of American art.

As one consequence, Remington was able to move his fine-art exhibitions to Knoedler's in New York City, a breakthrough for him into a much higher quality gallery. Five

paintings were sold during the 1906 show, one for $2,500. The reviews were of "a softened and harmonized Remington, looking as if he had been abroad studying. The shades of night help him to tones of mystery." The influence was not from abroad, but from his friend Childe Hassam, who was one of The Ten American Painters. Remington even bought acreage in Connecticut to be nearer the Impressionists.

On February 8, 1907, he "burned every old canvas in house today out on the snow" to clean his slate of realism. "About 75—and there is nothing left but my landscape studies." That was when *The Unknown Explorers* and *The Great American Explorers* series, except for *Radisson,* went up in satisfying smoke.

To Remington, the distasteful side of his career was still the work for *Collier's,* which reluctantly renewed his 1907 contract for another year. The magazine was continuing to insist on popular standards of violent Western action in daylight or classic Indian ritual. Accordingly, the editors professed to be pleased with *The Howl of the Weather* (plate 121) and *The Shadows at the Waterhole* (plate 123), while *Downing the Nigh Leader* (plate 122) and *Bringing Home the New Cook* (plate 124) were praised as high action. Remington felt compelled by his contract to paint these ultramasculine storytelling subjects, though he was no longer entirely comfortable doing them.

Figure 8. Compare with plate 122. [Richard F. Brush Art Gallery, St. Lawrence University]

Nevertheless, in 1907 *Collier's* published only six of the twelve paintings it had purchased, a sign of trouble ahead. One reason was that the style of the magazine was gradually changing from folksy realism to Art Nouveau. Maxfield Parrish was rising as the featured artist, while Remington and Gibson were in decline.

By today's standards, some of Remington's color paintings were poorly reproduced in *Collier's*. The halftone technique was new to the industry. The variation in quality could be substantial, judging by register, accuracy, and intensity of color. Sometimes one color plate failed to ink at all.

Special attention was given to producing the prints, which were truer to the original paintings than the reproductions in the magazine. Color was invariably a main attraction in the prints; the mature Remington never chose black and white to create a mood. Rich nocturnes with subtle darks were as close as he got. Even so, the plates could vary in register from print to print, and there were deviations in tonality (fig. 8).

Substantially all of Remington's 1907 pictures were made into prints, and they sold in larger numbers than ever before. *Collier's* exhorted its subscribers to "go to the best art, picture, book, stationery, or department store in your town and ask for these subjects. They have them, or, they can get them. Insist upon seeing them. If they will not furnish you with the pictures, we will send [them] to your address on receipt of price."

Many of the late Remington prints were tagged by *Collier's* with a corner card bearing a Remington signature simulated in ink and a claim that the print was an "artist's proof" (fig. 9). Actually, the "proofs" were not pulled by the artist before the press run, a requirement for an original print or artist's proof. The magazine acknowledged that "the continued demand for proofs of drawings by famous artists that appear in *Collier's* has led us to strike off from the original plates a number of proofs on heavy plate paper. These are printed with the greatest care and when framed present a very handsome appearance." Admittedly, the prints were made after the press run. The artists may never have seen them at any point in the production or marketing. The prints were not strictly "artist's proofs."

October 4, 1907, was Remington's forty-sixth birthday. *Pearson's Magazine* celebrated the day as his twenty-fifth anniversary as an artist, dating from the crumpled Wyoming sketch redrawn in *Harper's Weekly* for 1882. The magazine featured a letter from President Theodore Roosevelt asserting that Remington "is one of the most typical American artists we have had, and he has portrayed soldier, cowboy and rancher, Indian, horses and cattle of the plains for all time."

Remington was more pessimistic in looking back. He wrote, "My West passed out of existence so long ago as to make it merely a dream. It put on its hat, took up its blankets and marched off the board, the curtain came down and a new act was in progress." His sour mood was suited to the economic depression in the country. December 2, 1907, was the second Knoedler exhibition of his paintings. Only two of twelve were sold. Reviewers cited some of the action paintings initially done for *Collier's* as "blatantly, glaringly crude," while again praising the nocturnes the magazine sought to avoid.

Remington was beginning to notice that enthusiasm for his work was waning at *Collier's*. Will Bradley, who had become the art editor, favored the new European style that left little room for American Westerns. "Paintings returned by 'Sad Eyed Bradley' and 23 [skiddoo] for me," Remington groaned. "Begin to think of taking to the sage brush."

The only print that was issued after 1902 by a publisher other than *Collier's* was *The Last of His Race* (plate 127). The Chicago art dealer W. Scott Thurber had requested smaller paintings to sell for lower prices between exhibitions. Remington said, "I see the virtues of small pictures," and painted *The Last of His Race* for Chicago sales.

The print was produced as an oleograph, in oils on canvas rather than ink on paper. If it was a deliberate attempt to use a print to forge a Remington painting, it was the only instance while the artist was alive. The prints themselves have never been forged. They have not yet been valuable enough to justify the effort.

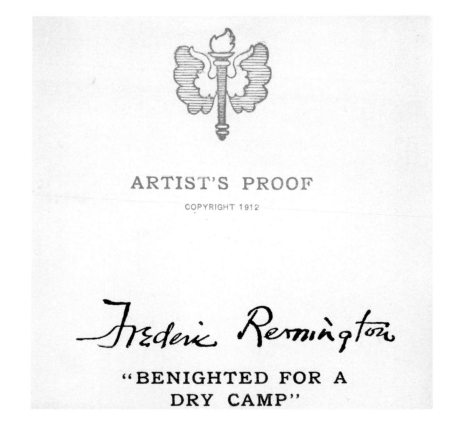

Figure 9. A simulated signature. [Authors' collection]

117.
The Parley
1906. "When the red man and the white were in parley, two dogs could not have bristled more nervously. They both feared treachery. There was wolf's law—behind it stood no honor code and the hand of peace was never far from the trigger."—*Collier's Weekly*, 10/29/1906, page 8 [Authors' collection]

116.
The Guard of the Whiskey Traders
1906. "Traders went to the Indians bearing strong water. This resulted in the death of the trader until the Indian understood that the trader must be protected so the Indians detailed camp-soldiers to strike any one who threatened the trader."—*Collier's Weekly*, 9/22/1906, page 8 [The Thomas Gilcrease Institute of American History and Art]

118.

***Lumber Camp at Night,
a.k.a. The Tragedy of
the Trees, Part I***

1906. Two months earlier, *Collier's* had warned its readers that "Mr. Remington has departed somewhat from his usual field and depicted in rather somber colors the life of the logging camp in a series of pictures 'The Tragedy of the Trees.'"
[The Thomas Gilcrease Institute of American History and Art]

119.
Snaking Logs to the Skidway, a.k.a. The Tragedy of the Trees, Part II

1906. According to the magazine caption, "This is the series of paintings by Mr. Remington presenting the epic of the forest—showing the story of man's conquest of the wooded wilderness. The lumbermen at work constitute the 'tragedy of the trees.' "—*Collier's Weekly,* 12/8/1906, page 8 [The Thomas Gilcrease Institute of American History and Art]

120.

Hauling Logs to the River, a.k.a. The Tragedy of the Trees, Part III

1907. *Collier's* saw the series as representing man's conquest of the wilderness, but this was not Remington's idea. He was an early conservationist who could not look at a Sunday newspaper without thinking of the forests destroyed to make the paper. [The Thomas Gilcrease Institute of American History and Art]

121.
The Howl of the Weather, a.k.a. The Squall

1907. On March 25, 1907, *Collier's* renewed its commitment to publish Remington's spreads for another year. Remington wrote, "Colliers gave me a contract $1000 a month and had big talk about the criticism—lunched Players." The magazine's complaints did not interfere with his eating.
[Authors' collection]

122.
Downing the Nigh Leader, a.k.a. The Attack

1907. Remington was amused by the acceptance of his paintings as fact. "Some well bred boys called," he remarked. "They take my pictures for veritable happenings & speculate on what will happen next to the puppets so arduous are boys' imaginations."
[Richard F. Brush Art Gallery, St. Lawrence University]

123.

**The Shadows at the
Waterhole**

1907. Robert Collier told
Remington to set his scenes
at noon. The painter compro-
mised in *The Shadows at the
Waterhole* by providing violent colors and hinting at the
action to come.
[Frederic Remington
Art Museum]

124.

**Bringing Home the
New Cook**

1907. Remington set aside
June and July to paint the
twelve pictures he had conceived and sketched for *Collier's* in the spring. In 1907
he was giving the magazine
the highest order of Western
art, but the editors still withheld six from publication.
[Authors' collection]

125.
The Scouts

1908. This is another precursor of the 1909 compositions, posed and devoid of direct action or storytelling. Yet *The Scouts* suggests that something is going on outside the frame of the picture, just beyond what the viewer can see.
[Frederic Remington Art Museum]

126.
The Ceremony of the Scalps

1908. In July 1907 Remington observed, "My Scalp Ceremony back, & impossible. My improvement has put it on the bum." He was too pessimistic. Further changes made the painting so successful that it was reproduced as this print.
[Frederic Remington Art Museum]

127.
The Last of His Race, a.k.a. The Vanishing American, a.k.a. The Last American

1908. The treatment is typical of Remington's later style of fine art in that the emphasis is on mood rather than action. The print looks like a painting, oil on canvas, and is roughly the same size as the original it is frequently mistaken for.
[Frederic Remington Art Museum]

The Impressionist Artist

The Grass Fire
(plate 129, detail)

Although Remington frequently made himself out to be a cowboy unschooled in matters concerning art, he was really *au courant*. In 1908, he was in the midst of the New York City art ferment, visiting museums and galleries, attending lectures, and discussing techniques with critics and other leading painters.

Allying himself with The Ten, he recognized that "painting is now in its infancy. Small canvases are best—all plein air color and outlines lost." Still growing as a painter, he acknowledged that "I am learning to use Prussian [blue in nocturnes] and Ultramarine. I have *now* discovered for the first time how to do the *silver sheen* of moonlight."

His complaint was, "I feel I am trying to do the impossible in not having a chance to work direct [from nature] but as there are no such people as I paint its 'studio' or

nothing." As a compromise, he painted some backgrounds on location in the West and then added the figures after he returned home.

He could not make himself conform to the nouveau style of curlicues and mythology at *Collier's*. Three-quarters of his magazine pieces during this period were nocturnes or scenes in subdued daylight, while his pictures were edging more toward symbolism.

On June 29, 1908, *Collier's* severed its relationship with the artist as of the end of the year. Remington said he was glad to see the arrangement terminate, but the finish was not of his volition.

After he was free of *Collier's*, action was anathema in his art. He was pleased with his pictures when they were "quite vibrating and good tone." Painting was "an expression of light," and his canvas was intended to "glow and quiver until it seems to exude the palpitating quality which light holds."

He left for Wyoming on September 8. "Such is the life of an artist in search of the beautiful," he claimed, but he was old for forty-seven. He could not ride a horse, eat camp food, sleep on a cot, walk a trail, tolerate altitude, or climb into an upper berth.

On December 1, 1908, a pivotal Knoedler show opened. Even though most of the paintings were the final year's submissions to *Collier's, The New York Times* reported that "the types of Western character are like what we see in imagination when we call to mind a Western scene." The *New York Globe* wrote, "Remington sounds a purely American note. His color is purer and his figures are more in atmosphere."

Seven of the thirteen paintings sold the first week. Among those sold were *With the Eye of the Mind* (plate 130), *The Grass Fire* (plate 129), and *Stampeded by Lightning* (plate 142), about which he bragged, "I have always wanted to be able to paint running horses so you would feel the details and not see them. I am getting so I can stagger at it." He told himself, "I have landed among the painters and well up to[o]."

With the Eye of the Mind was one of Remington's most powerful compositions. The cloud formations suggesting threatening gods interacted with the superstitious figures. The menace from the sky was an overt and integral part of the picture.

Even the horses in the painting registered awe.

While sophisticated Europeans such as Gauguin, Cézanne, and Van Gogh sometimes depicted a hidden demonic face woven into a backdrop to provide a covert threat to a peaceful scene, Remington and the American Impressionists did not use subliminal secondary images.

Despite the approbation from the critics, Remington was not yet entirely certain of his place in the art world. He observed that "a man wants to sell my early painting 'The Missionary.' Thus my early enemies come to haunt me. I am helpless. I would buy them all if I were able and burn them up." He had destroyed sixteen more paintings on January 25, 1908. A third burning took place on December 19, 1908, and a fourth on February 15, 1909. He relished the burnings because he believed he was protecting his reputation. He did not comprehend that he was already an American master. Every piece he painted was important because each showed that his first influences were not European but American and self-generated.

It seemed to him that one wonderful event was following another in his life. He was described as "an artistic personality that is always pressing forward." At the December 4, 1909, Knoedler exhibition, six paintings were sold the first night. The reviewers wrote that "Remington's work is splendid in its technique, epic in its imaginative qualities, and historically important."

Remington gloated, "The art critics have all 'come down'—I have splendid notes from all the papers. They ungrudgingly give me a high place. The 'illustrator' phase has become back ground." He added, "I was never so happy."

On December 18, 1909, just two weeks after his triumph at Knoedler's, he said he "wrenched" a stomach muscle. On the twentieth, he had intense pains in his belly. On the twenty-second, doctors examined him. The next day they operated on him on the table in his kitchen. His appendix had burst and septic peritonitis had set in. There was no hope.

He died December 26, 1909. His gravestone was plain. He had wanted "He Knew the Horse" inscribed on it, but his wife refused. She would have to lie next to him.

128.
The Warrior's Last Ride
1908. The colors and the subject were not what *Collier's* wanted, except for the sky. By the end of July, Remington had shipped only eight paintings to the magazine. Six were accepted, one was returned "for corrections," and one was refused "for keeps."
[Authors' collection]

129.

***The Grass Fire, a.k.a.
Backfiring***

1909. Remington said that
grass fires were "effective in
open country where chances
of surprising a watchful enemy were small." His diary
entry for April 4, 1908, read,
"Worked on 'Grass Fire'—a
new moon. Firelight and
moon—very difficult."
[Frederic Remington
Art Museum]

130.

With the Eye of the Mind

1909. *With the Eye of the
Mind* was judged one of the
two best paintings in Remington's 1908 show. The art critics were enthusiastic, praising
him for "fierce themes han-
dled with audacity and amaz-
ing vigor of expression. His
pictures are great."
[Authors' collection]

131.
The Quarrel

1909. In August 1909, *Collier's* had a stockpile of Remington paintings and was publishing them in a sequence intelligible only to the editors. *The Quarrel* had been exhibited in 1907. The painting filled the magazine's bill, but critics panned it as poor art.

[Authors' collection]

132.
Indians Simulating Buffalo

1909. The background is badlands, a rare specificity of landscape for Remington. The subject is a record of historical Indian practices, a gentler George Catlin type of ethnological theme rather than the violent or melodramatic incident *Collier's* preferred.

[Authors' collection]

133.
On the Southern Plains in 1860, a.k.a. *The Cavalry Charge*

1909. These are familiar multiple galloping military figures, but this time the print shows the heavy impasto of the original painting which was exhibited in 1907. Rather than the cavalry Remington preferred, Indians were his most common subjects.

[Authors' collection]

134.
The Sentinel

1909. In the exhibition including *The Sentinel,* night
scenes were "a great stride
forward. [The] study of
moonlight appears to have
reacted on the grain of his
art, so that in drawing, brush
work, color, atmosphere, he
has achieved greater freedom
and breadth."
[Authors' collection]

Postmortem

The Longhorn Cattle Sign
(plate 144, detail)

The long relationship between *Collier's* and Remington was a boon for the artist's public. During the last decade, eighty of his works were reproduced in color in the magazine and sixty-five of them were also made into color prints ready for framing. An additional seven prints were in black and white.

In contrast, over the twenty-one years of his career when he painted more than two thousand pictures in black and white and color for an array of other publishers, only seventy-five became prints. Moreover, almost half of those earlier reproductions were in three lengthy series: the Miles illustrations, *The Way of an Indian* illustrations, and *A Bunch of Buckskins.*

When Remington died, however, *Collier's* gave limited space to its perfunctory

funereal coverage in the January 8, 1910, issue. The magazine did not beat its figurative breast in a lavish display of grief. After all, *Collier's* owned the publication rights to another seventeen fine paintings that might have been diminished in value by the demise of the artist. Instead of a lengthy sobbing, paintings were reproduced and prints and articles appeared as if he were still alive. This continued for four years, until the magazine ran out of its pictorial inventory.

In retrospect, these late *Collier's* prints were his true masterpieces, as well as the bridge to his more refined artistic endeavors of 1909. *A Cavalry Charge* (plate 138), *The Call for Help* (plate 140), *The Buffalo Hunter* (plate 145), and *In from the Night Herd* (plate 147) were among the most dynamic and the most poignant prints.

When the last Remington painting was reproduced in *Collier's* in 1913, there was no further publication of his work in the magazine. Even the inventory of his jigsaw puzzles was closed out: "The Idle Hour Picture Puzzles contain famous pictures by Remington. Puzzles containing 150 pieces regular price $1.50. Price now 75 cents." In place of his illustrations, figures were posed to simulate such compositions as *A Post Office in the "Cow Country"* (plate 65) and run in the magazine as photographic illustrations. Photography and Art Nouveau were in vogue.

There was no massive public demand to bring back Remington's pictures. Interest was suspended for the moment. *Collier's* ceased its production of Remington prints, although other publishers including museums have continued to issue his prints to this day.

Remington's aura as a master painter faded after his death. One reason was the short term of his reign. He received his greatest critical accolades in December 1909, and he died the same month. Another reason was that the West as a subject had saturated the market. His mantle passed to Charley Russell. Many Western buffs preferred Russell because he was a real Westerner and a simpler good ol' boy with slimmer pretensions toward immortality.

In 1888, Remington had invented a phony biography to de-emphasize his insignificant Yale and Art Students League studies in favor of trumped-up Western experiences as cowboy and Indian scout. Today, when he is again accepted as an American master, scholars and critics justify their praise of his work on the grounds that his Yale art training was invaluable to him. The schooling was, they say, only once removed from the traditions of classical French master painters. In reality, a teacher who might have spoken to him in New Haven had a brother who was studying in Paris.

Insecure as Remington was about his substantial contribution to American art, he would have loved the current raves, regardless of the attempted denial of his all-American background. How he arrived on top meant very little to him compared to being there.

135.

Buying Polo Ponies in the West, a.k.a. Horse Muster

1910. Remington died in 1909, but his paintings lingered on in *Collier's*. As an oddity, this print is in black and white rather than in color, as other *Collier's* prints had been since 1901. Reproduction in the magazine was in color.
[Amon Carter Museum]

136.

The Navajo Raid

1910. The painting was exhibited in 1907. The subject dates back to the first half of the nineteenth century. The Navajos are known now as sheepherders and artisans, but then they were frequent raiders of other New Mexican villages and pueblos.
[Frederic Remington Art Museum]

137.

Shotgun Hospitality

1910. "When Indians called in at the camp-fire of a lone white man they might do no worse than eat his grub, but the preliminaries were apt to make the host nervous."

—*Collier's Weekly,*

9/17/1910, page 12. In 1908 critics noted, "The Indians in 'Shot-gun Hospitality' are true [Fenimore] Cooper 'braves.' " [Frederic Remington Art Museum]

138.
***A Cavalry Charge, a.k.a.
The Charge, a.k.a. The
Revolver Charge***
1910. This is the last of many
cavalry charges Remington
painted. Despite Remington's
brief lapse after the Spanish-
American War, he thought
the cavalry was the most
romantic of the armed
forces. His father had been
a heroic cavalry colonel.
[Frederic Remington
Art Museum]

139.
The Pool in the Desert
1910. This was exhibited in
1908 as *The Water Hole, Na-
vajoes*. The composition was
designed for beauty, with
the shadows of the figures
pointing toward the small
water hole at the lower left.
For a tight focus, *Collier's*
cropped both the pool and
the signature.
[Authors' collection]

140.
The Call for Help, a.k.a. *At Bay*

1910. The caption read, "Wolves hesitate to bring on an engagement so near." —*Collier's Weekly,* 12/17/1910, page 6. The print received another criticism from Charley Russell: "When a horse is scared, it runs. Besides, there never were horses ascared of any God damn wolves that lived in Montana." [Authors' collection, tear sheet]

141.
The Snow Trail

1911. Remington had been dead for more than a year by 1911, but *Collier's* was still running feature articles about his boyhood, using his paintings as illustrations and prints, and selling jigsaw puzzles of his work. This was a 1908 painting. [Authors' collection]

142.

Stampeded by Lightning,
a.k.a. *The Stampede*

1911. The caption read,
"Lightning has started a herd
of cattle, and cowboys are
trying to head them off."
—*Collier's Weekly,*
2/18/1911, page 8. The painting is frequently cited to
show how Remington used
photographs to depict the
gallop. Photographs are
static, however, compared to
Remington's vivid motion.
[Frederic Remington
Art Museum]

143.

**Benighted for a
Dry Camp**

1911. The painting was exhibited in 1907 as *The Dry
Camp*. It represents the artist's move toward Impressionism while holding to Western
subject matter. The frontiers-
man is not quite "benighted,"
however. The blinding sun
has not yet set.

[Authors' collection]

144.

The Longhorn Cattle Sign

1911. According to the caption, "A cowboy indicates that a herd of cattle is approaching and the Indian is answering that he is willing that the herd should cross the reservation."—*Collier's Weekly,* 5/6/1911, page 8. Modern critics see this as "one of Remington's most powerful pieces." [Frederic Remington Art Museum]

145.

The Buffalo Hunter, a.k.a. The Buffalo Runner

1911. There is a similar vertical painting titled *Episode of a Buffalo Hunt.* The conjecture is that the vertical painting's shape was unsuited for a *Collier's* frontispiece. Remington painted this horizontal picture as a replacement and saved the vertical picture for his show. [The Library of Congress]

146.

The Dead Men, a.k.a.
The Discovery

1911. "French half-breeds
have come upon evidences of
a fight," the caption
explained. "Had they been
white men, they would have
been merely curious, and had
they been Indians they never
would have slackened pace to
look at the gruesome
sight."—*Collier's Weekly,*
9/9/1911, page 8
[Authors' collection]

In from the Night Herd

1912. The painting was exhibited in 1908. Remington had learned early on to select provocative titles such as this one. Despite the resulting confusion, he did not object to repeating titles he found successful. He first used *In from the Night Herd* in 1888, the year of his first print.

[Authors' collection]

148.

Cutting Out Pony Herds, a.k.a. The Stampede

1913. With this cover, *Collier's* ended its reproduction of Remington's art. What had started with fanfare ended in silence. Photographs had replaced paintings as illustrations in the magazine, Art Nouveau had deposed Impressionism, and the West had lost out for the moment.

[Frederic Remington Art Museum]

In the Final Analysis

In from the Night Herd
(plate 147, detail)

One key to Remington's art was his respect for male Indians as warriors. He saw them as worthy savages, not anglicized or noble or spiritual or, on the other hand, vile. To him they were natural men.

He recognized too that the Indians were here first. Their presence was necessary to allow him to make heroes out of the invading soldiers. Yet he pictured Indians as losing the plains wars only because of the army's technological advantages. If he had had his way, he would have embraced Indians by enlisting them in an irregular regiment of the United States Cavalry.

In the beginning of his career, Remington depicted Indians as valiant participants in the bloody history of their defense against white encroachment. In the end he made

them mystical. He was concerned with their essential Indianness in his writing and his art, but they were neither friends nor pets who were expected to know their place.

For him, the frontiersmen, the Indians, the army of the West, and the Tex-Mex cowboys all went off the stage at about the same time. By 1890, the frontiersmen had disappeared with the frontier. The defeated Indians were retired to the dreariness of their reservations. The Indian-fighting army had no one left to fight in the West, and the cowboys nursed cows behind fences.

Although Remington was prudent in his life, he was adventurous in his art. When he was induced by peer pressure to remove narration from his pictures, he deliberately abandoned the niche where he had combined Western action with Impressionism in ways his contemporaries could not match. He who had been the pacesetter willingly risked becoming just one of the boys in symbolism—albeit a uniquely American boy featuring his special Old West characters. He also left printmaking behind, if simply because no publisher sought publication rights.

He was a restless man of many talents. In 1909 he was painting landscapes of the Adirondacks as well as looking for new media—monuments and murals. If he had lived, he might have tried original graphics, too. Members of The Ten American Painters such as Weir, Chase, Benson, Hassam, and Twachtman all made serious essays at original prints. That was their change of pace in art.

Remington's change was sculpture, which might have led him to become more aware of comparisons between hands-on modeling and engraving. He would probably have noted the moneymaking possibilities in original multiples on paper, as he did multiples in bronze.

In the end, though, the irony is that by 1909 he was ashamed of the storytelling qualities of most of the pictures that had become prints. He would have destroyed all of these original paintings if he could have. He was wrong in his artistic judgment; great artists such as Remington do not have to deny the past. In fact, many people today think more highly of some of the paintings he burned than of those he preserved.

To him, however, these older paintings represented only his illustrations, the compromising commercial exploitations he came to hate. That was his ultimate error, responding to the tenets of the day as if he was a master just for the moment instead of for all time.

Appendixes

APPENDIX A
Alphabetized List of Remington Prints

Admiring Eyes Followed White Otter, see *Nothing but Cheerful Looks Followed the Bat*

Advance Guard, see *On the March—the Advance Guard*

After the Skirmish, see *Soldiers Opening Their Own Veins for Want of Water*

Antelope Hunting, color, Gould, 1889 (plate 7)

Argument with the Town Marshal, An, color, *Collier's Weekly,* 2/11/1905 (plate 98)

Arizona Cowboy, An, color, *A Bunch of Buckskins,* 1901 (plate 73)

Army Mail Ambulance, An—A "Busted" Brake and a Down Grade, sepia, *Harper's Weekly,* 9/20/1890 (plate 13)

Army Packer, An, a.k.a. *A Regular,* color, *A Bunch of Buckskins,* 1901 (plate 72)

At Bay, see *The Call for Help*

At Last, see *Killing a Cattle Thief*

Attack, The, see both *Downing the Nigh Leader* and *Sioux Warriors*

Attacking the Indian Chief, "Crazy Horse," see *The Crazy Horse Fight*

Attack on an Overland Coach, An, see *An Overland Station*

Backfiring, see *The Grass Fire*

Before the Warning Scream of the Shrapnel, see *Scream of the Shrapnel*

Bell Mare, The, a.k.a. *In the Enemy's Country,* color, *Collier's Weekly,* 8/13/1904 (plate 93)

Benighted for a Dry Camp, color, *Collier's Weekly,* 3/4/1911 (plate 143)

Black-foot Brave, A, see *A Cheyenne Buck*

Branding Cattle (An Incident of Ranch Life), sepia, Muir, 1888 (plate 2)

Breed, A, a.k.a. *An Indian Scout,* a.k.a. *A North-west Half Breed,* color, *A Bunch of Buckskins,* 1901 (plate 69)

Bringing Home the New Cook, color, *Collier's Weekly,* 11/2/1907 (plate 124)

Bucking Bronco, A, black and white, The Century Co., 1888 (plate 5)

Buffalo Hunter, The, a.k.a. *The Buffalo Runner,* color, *Collier's Weekly,* 7/1/1911 (plate 145)

Buffalo Runner, The, see *The Buffalo Hunter*

Buffalo Runners, The, color, *Collier's Weekly,* 6/17/1905 (plate 103)

Burning a Refuge, see *Indians Firing the Prairie*

"Busted" Brake and a Down Grade, A, see *An Army Mail Ambulance*

Buying Polo Ponies in the West, a.k.a. *Horse Muster,* black and white, *Collier's Weekly,* 3/5/1910 (plate 135)

Call for Help, The, a.k.a. *At Bay,* color, *Collier's Weekly,* 12/17/1910 (plate 140)

Calling the Moose, a.k.a. *Calling to the Moose,* a.k.a. *Calling to Death,* sepia, *Collier's Weekly,* 10/12/1901, but full color as artist's proof (plate 66)

Calling to Death, see *Calling the Moose*

Calling to the Moose, see *Calling the Moose*

Canada Goose Shooting, see *Goose Shooting*

Captain Baldwin Hunting the Hostile Camp, a.k.a. *Hunting the Hostile Camp,* a.k.a. *Scouting Party,* black and white, Werner, 1898 (plate 38)

Captive, The, see *Missing*

Caught in the Circle, color, *Collier's Weekly,* 12/7/1901 (plate 75)

Cavalry Charge, A, a.k.a. *The Charge,* a.k.a. *The Revolver Charge,* color, *Collier's Weekly,* 10/8/1910 (plate 138)

Cavalry Charge, The, see *On the Southern Plains in 1860*

(Cavalryman), see *The Cossack Post*

Cavalry Officer, A, color, *A Bunch of Buckskins,* 1901 (plate 71)

Ceremony of the Fastest Horse, The, a.k.a. *Over the Prairie Fled White Otter with His Stolen Bride,* color, *The Way of an Indian,* 1906 (1900) (plate 57)

Ceremony of the Scalps, The, color, *Collier's Weekly,* 6/13/1908 (plate 126)

Change of Ownership, A, see *The Stampede*

Charge, The, see *A Cavalry Charge*

Charge of Roman Nose, The, see *Forsythe's Fight on the Republican River, 1868*

Charge of the Rough Riders, The, black and white, R. H. Russell, 1899 (plate 44)

Charge on the Sun-pole, The, see *Sioux Indians Charging the Sun-pole*

Cheyenne Buck, A, a.k.a. *An Indian Brave,*

APPENDIX B
List of Plates

Sources

ACM: The Amon Carter Museum, Fort Worth, TX 76107-2631.

Buf: The Whitney Gallery of Western Art, Buffalo Bill Historical Center, Cody, WY 82414.

Cow: National Cowboy Hall of Fame and Western Heritage Center, Oklahoma City, OK 73111.

Den: Western History Department, Denver Public Library, Denver, CO 80203-2165.

Gil: The Thomas Gilcrease Institute of American History and Art, Tulsa, OK 74127.

Gund: The Gund Collection of Western Art, Princeton, NJ 08542-0449.

LoC: Prints and Photographs Division, The Library of Congress, Washington, DC 20540.

Myr: Richard Myers, Canton, NY 13617.

Nor: The R. W. Norton Art Gallery, Shreveport, LA 71106-1899.

RAM: The Frederic Remington Art Museum, Ogdensburg, NY 13669.

Roc: The Rockwell Museum, Corning, NY 14830.

Sam: The authors, Peggy and Harold Samuels, Corrales, NM 87048.

S&W: Smith & Wesson, Springfield, MA 01102-2208.

StL: The Richard F. Brush Art Gallery, St. Lawrence University, Canton, NY 13617.

Plates

1. *Mule Train Crossing the Sierras,* illustrated opposite p. 28 in John Muir's *Picturesque California.* The J. Dewing Company, San Francisco, 1888. Black-and-white photogravure. Image 8″ × 10½″. Page size 14″ × 19″ in portfolios for limited edition, 12½″ × 16½″ in trade edition, 11″ × 14¼″ in bound two volumes. Reproduced on board; some on satin, 10½″ × 14½″ or larger. Signed lower center: REMINGTON. Collections: Sam, Gil, StL, RAM, ACM.

2. *Branding Cattle (An Incident of Ranch Life),* same origin as above but opposite p. 184. Sepia. Image 6½″ × 10″. Signed lower right: Remington. Collections: Sam, RAM, ACM.

3. *Miners Prospecting for Gold,* same origin as above but opposite p. 236. Overall blue tone; sometimes gray-green. Image 7¾″ × 10¼″. Signed lower right: REMINGTON. Collections: Sam, LoC, RAM, ACM.

4. *A Navajo Sheep-Herder,* same origin as above but opposite p. 320. Black and white. Image 8″ × 11¼″. Signed lower left: REMINGTON. Collections: Sam and ACM (print on satin), RAM.

5. *A Bucking Bronco,* from Theodore Roosevelt's *Ranch Life and the Hunting Trail,* The Century Co., New York, 1888. Recopyrighted 1908 as a 14″ × 9½″ black-and-white reproduction by Copley Prints, Curtis and Cameron, Boston. Signed lower right: F. Remington. Collection: LoC.

6. *Dragging a Bull's Hide Over a Prairie Fire in Northern Texas,* "Supplement to *Harper's Weekly,* October 27, 1888," stated on top margin of black-and-white double-page wood engraving. Image 14¾″ × 20½″, on paper 16″ × 22″. No printing on reverse. Bound in issue with tape so as to be removable for framing, but necessarily folded once. Signed lower right: FREDERIC REMINGTON. Collection: Sam.

7. *Antelope Hunting,* from portfolio edited by A. C. Gould titled *Sport: or Shooting and Fishing,* Bradless, Whidden Publishing Co., Boston, 1889. Page size 17¼″ × 23¾″. Paper is double layer with gauze in between. Chromolithograph has embossed texture within 12″ × 18″ image. First Remington print in color. Signed lower left: Frederic Remington—89. Collections: Sam, RAM, ACM.

8. *Goose Shooting,* a.k.a. *Canada Goose Shooting,* a.k.a. *Pheasant Shooting,* same ori-

gin and size as above. Second Remington print in color. Signed lower left: —FREDERIC REMINGTON—. Collections: Sam, RAM, ACM.

9. *Hiawatha and the Pearl-Feather,* a.k.a. *An Indian Battle,* published as an illustration in Henry Wadsworth Longfellow's *The Song of Hiawatha,* Houghton Mifflin Co., Boston, 1890. Copyright notice on lower left by Copley Prints, Curtis and Cameron, Boston, 1903. Sepia photogravure. Vertical sizes 9½″ × 6¾″, 13⅜″ × 9½″, and 19⅞″ × 14⅛″. Signed lower right: FREDERIC REMINGTON. Collection: LoC.

10. *Hiawatha's Wedding Feast,* a.k.a. *An Indian Dance,* same book and print publishers and same approximate horizontal print sizes as above. Signed lower left: FREDERIC REMINGTON. Collection: LoC.

11. *Picture-Writing,* same book and print publishers and same approximate horizontal sizes as above. Signed lower right: FREDERIC REMINGTON. Collection: LoC.

12. *The Hunting of Pau-Puk-Keewis,* a.k.a. *An Indian Runner,* same book and print publishers and same approximate vertical sizes as above. Signed lower center: FREDERIC REMINGTON. Collection: LoC.

13. *An Army Mail Ambulance—A "Busted" Brake and a Down Grade,* issued as double-page supplement to *Harper's Weekly,* 9/20/1890. Sepia photoengraving, print size 19⅞″ × 12½″. Signed lower right center: REMINGTON; faintly lower right: KURTZ [engraver]. Collection: Sam.

14. *On the Cattle Range—"What's the Show For a Christmas Dinner, Chief?"* issued as a double-page supplement to *Harper's Weekly,* 12/20/1890. Black-and-white photoengrav-

ing, print size 13¾″ × 19¾″. Signed lower right: —FREDERIC REMINGTON—. Collection: Sam.

15. *A Dash for the Timber,* published in 1890 by The Gravure Etching Company as black-and-white photoengraving, size 15″ × 26″. Also published in sepia, size 4½″ × 8″ copyrighted 1898, 8⅜″ × 15⅜″ in 1916, and 13½″ × 23½″ in 1917 by A. W. Elson & Co., Boston. Published about 1899 by R. H. Russell as a black-and-white platinum print size 16″ × 29″ on 24″ × 36″ mat. Signed lower left: FREDERIC REMINGTON, and again manually lower right. Collection: Gund.

16. *On the March—The Advance Guard,* a.k.a. *Advance Guard,* published as an illustration in "General Miles's Indian Campaigns," *The Century Magazine,* July 1891. Issued as a sepia photogravure by Curtis and Cameron, Boston, in 1902, sizes 6⅛″ × 9½″ and 13″ × 20¼″. Signed lower left: Frederic Remington. Collection: LoC.

17. *A Fantasy from the Pony War Dance,* illustrated in black and white in Julian Ralph's "Chartering a Nation," *Harper's Monthly,* December 1891. Print is in color. Size 7″ × 7¼″. Signed lower right: FREDERIC REMINGTON; lower left: F. S. KING [engraver]. Collection: Sam tear sheet.

18. *A Russian Cossack,* from a sketch made in Warsaw, laid in Part Two of a portfolio, *American Illustrators,* by F. Hopkinson Smith, Charles Scribner's Sons, New York, 1892. Page size 17″ × 13″. Color plate size 10½″ × 8¾″. Signed catercorner lower left: Frederic Remington. Collections: Sam, RAM, ACM.

19. *Moving the Led Horses,* a.k.a. *Dismounted—The Fourth Troopers Moving*

the Led Horses, published in *The Century Magazine,* January 1892. Black-and-white image 5″ × 8″ on paper 13½″ × 17½″, proof plate from folio folder *The Century Gallery—Selected Proofs from The Century and St. Nicholas Magazine,* The Century Co., New York, 1893. Signed lower left: FREDERIC REMINGTON. Collection: Sam.

20. *Sioux Indians Charging the Sun-pole,* a.k.a. *The Charge on the Sun-pole,* same folio and approximate size as above. Published as illustration in *The Century Magazine,* March 1890. Signed lower left: F. REMINGTON; lower right: EVANS [engraver]. Collection: Gil.

21. *Mounting a Wild One,* published in *Harper's Monthly,* March 1894, page 521. Black-and-white lithograph 23″ × 13″ by Davis & Sanford. Signed lower left: Frederic Remington, the late form of signature, and dated 1894. Copyright Harper Brothers. Collection: Sam tear sheet.

22. *A Running Bucker,* published in 1895 by Davis & Sanford as a black-and-white lithograph, 20″ × 16″. Image size 15″ × 11″. Also 10¾ × 9″. Signed lower left: Frederic Remington, the late form of signature. Collection: StL.

23. *A "Sunfisher,"* same as above. Signature lower center in late style. Collections: StL, Gil.

24. *An Indian Soldier,* black and white, print size 10″ × 12½″, copyright 1897 by R. H. Russell. Also in brown and white as signed artist's proof in some copies of deluxe edition of *Drawings,* R. H. Russell, New York, 1897. Signed lower right. Collection: ACM photo-lithograph.

25. *Cow Pony Pathos,* black and white, image

9″ × 13½″, copyright 1897 by R. H. Russell. Reprinted from *Drawings*. Signed lower right and again in the margin. Collection: ACM photolithograph.

26. *An Overland Station—Indians Coming in with the Stage,* a.k.a. *Indians Coming in with the Stage,* a.k.a. *An Attack on an Overland Coach,* brown and white lithograph, 7¼″ × 9½″, copyright 1897 by R. H. Russell. Reprinted from *Drawings*. Signed lower right. Collection: ACM.

27. *A Misdeal,* a.k.a. *A Miss Deal,* black-and-white print, 12″ × 16½″, copyright 1897 by R. H. Russell. Reprinted from *Drawings*. Signed lower right. Collection: ACM photolithograph.

28. *Solitude,* black-and-white print, image 8½″ × 12½″, copyright 1897 by R. H. Russell. Reprinted from *Drawings*. Signed lower right. Collection: Gil.

29. *A Citadel on the Plains,* black-and-white print, image 8½″ × 13½″, copyright 1897 by R. H. Russell. Reprinted from *Drawings*. Signed lower right. Collection: Gil.

30. *Sioux Warriors,* a.k.a. *The Attack,* black-and-white photogravure, size 16″ × 23″. One of fourteen prints in undated folder, *Rotogravure,* published by The Werner Co., Akron, Ohio, about 1898. Also bound in the book *Frontier Sketches,* published by Werner in 1898. Also sepia print, copyright 1907 by W. D. Harney, Racine, Wisconsin. Signed lower right. Collections: Roc, LoC.

31. *Soldiers Opening Their Own Veins for Want of Water,* a.k.a. *After the Skirmish,* second of fourteen black-and-white prints from same folder. Also in black and white by Har-

ney. Signed lower right. Collections: Roc, Gil, LoC.

32. *Indian Village Routed,* a.k.a. *Troop Surprising a Camp,* third of fourteen black-and-white prints from same folder. Also in black and white by Harney. Signed lower right. Collections: Roc, LoC.

33. *Twenty-five to One,* a.k.a. *The Last Stand,* fourth of fourteen black-and-white prints from same folder. Also in sepia by Harney. Signed lower right. Collections: Roc, LoC, Gil.

34. *General Miles Envoy to the Hostiles on the Staked Plain,* a.k.a. *Indian Winter Encampment on the Staked Plain,* a.k.a. *When Winter Is Cruel,* vaulted top, fifth of fourteen black-and-white prints from same folder. Signed lower right. Collection: Gil.

35. *Meeting between the Lines,* a.k.a. *The Parley,* also with the addition of *"God Almighty Made Me an Indian, and Not an Agency Indian,"* sixth of fourteen black-and-white prints from the same folder. Also in sepia by Harney. Signed lower right. Collections: Roc, LoC.

36. *Indians Firing the Prairie,* a.k.a. *Burning a Refuge,* vaulted top, seventh of fourteen black-and-white prints from same folder. Also in sepia by Harney. Signed lower left. Collections: Roc, LoC, Gil.

37. *Pursuing the Indians,* a.k.a. *Guarding the Supply Train,* vaulted top, eighth of fourteen black-and-white prints from same folder. Also in black and white by Harney. Signed lower right. Collections: Roc, LoC.

38. *Captain Baldwin Hunting the Hostile Camp,* a.k.a. *Hunting the Hostile Camp,* a.k.a.

Scouting Party, Ninth of fourteen black-and-white prints from same folder. Also in sepia by Harney. Signed lower right. Collections: Roc, LoC.

39. *The Crazy Horse Fight,* a.k.a. *Attacking the Indian Chief, "Crazy Horse,"* tenth of fourteen black-and-white prints from same folder. Signed lower right. Collections: Roc, Gil.

40. *The Lame Deer Fight,* eleventh of fourteen black-and-white prints from same folder. Signed lower right. Collections: Roc, Gil.

41. *Mounting the Infantry on Captured Ponies,* twelfth of fourteen black-and-white prints from same folder. Signed lower right. Collections: Roc, Gil.

42. *Fighting over the Captured Herd,* a.k.a. *Fighting over a Stolen Herd,* a.k.a. *Protecting the Herd,* thirteenth of fourteen black-and-white prints from same folder. Also in sepia by Harney. Signed lower right. Collections: Roc, LoC.

43. *Surrender of Chief Joseph,* a.k.a. *The Truce,* also with the addition of *"From Where the Sun Now Stands I Fight No More against the White Man,"* fourteenth of fourteen black-and-white prints from the same folder. Also in sepia by Harney. Signed lower center. Collections: Roc, LoC.

44. *The Charge of the Rough Riders,* black-and-white platinum print, 16″ × 29″ on mat 24″ × 36″, published by R. H. Russell for sale at ten dollars, probably in 1899. Signed lower right. Collection: RAM.

45. *Missing,* a.k.a. *The Captive,* also platinum print from Russell. Image 16″ × 27½″ on board 24″ × 36″ or 26¾″ × 38″. Signed

lower right. Collection: RAM.

46. *Scream of the Shrapnel,* a.k.a. *Before the Warning Scream of the Shrapnel,* also platinum print from Russell. The painting was for Remington's article "With the Fifth Corps" in *Harper's Monthly,* November 1898. Signed below the path lower right. Collection: Sam tear sheet.

47. *Questionable Companionship,* also platinum print from Russell. Full-page 9″ × 13″ line drawing in *Harper's Weekly,* 8/9/1890. Signed lower left: FREDERIC REMINGTON. Collection: Sam tear sheet.

48. *Forsythe's Fight on the Republican River, 1868,* also with *The Charge of Roman Nose.* Platinum print from Russell, 14½″ × 28½″, first published in *Drawings.* Signed lower right. Collection: RAM.

49. *Half-Breed Horse Thieves of the Northwest,* black-and-white print also from Russell, image 8½″ × 13½″. First published in *Drawings.* Signed lower right. Collection: Gil.

50. *A First-Class Fighting Man,* published in *Collier's Weekly* in double-page black-and-white spread 3/25/1899. Also a black-and-white "artist's proof" printed on heavy plate paper, 22″ × 16″ with self-borders, offered 8/12/1899 for fifty cents from *Collier's.* Signed large, lower right. Collection: Sam tear sheet.

51. *A Crow Scout,* black-and-white print, size 10″ × 12½″, copyright 1900 by R. H. Russell. Also in umber ink, size 6⅜ × 8⅝″. From *Drawings.* Signed lower right. Collections: ACM, LoC.

52. *O Gray Wolf of My Clan, Shall We Have Fortune?* one of nine color prints sized about 9″ × 14″ taken from Remington's novel, *The Way of an Indian,* published by Fox Duffield & Company, New York, 1906. Prints published by McConnell Printing Co., New York, as supplements to the *Chicago Examiner,* 1906. Signed lower right. Collections: Myr, Gil.

53. *Pretty Mother of the Night—White Otter Is No Longer a Boy,* second of nine color prints from the novel, but smaller than the others at 11½″ × 9″. Signed lower right. At lower left is "Supplement to Chicago Examiner." Collection: Myr.

54. *The Interpreter Waved at the Naked Youth, Sitting There on His War-Pony,* a.k.a. *The Interpreter Pointed to White Otter on His War-Pony,* published in *Cosmopolitan* in black and white with a golden overlay, third of nine color prints from the novel. Signed lower right. Collection: Myr.

55. *I Will Tell the White Man How He Can Have His Ponies Back,* a.k.a. *White Otter Defies the White Man,* fourth of nine color prints from the novel. Signed lower right. Collection: Myr.

56. *Nothing but Cheerful Looks Followed the Bat,* a.k.a. *Admiring Eyes Followed White Otter,* fifth of nine color prints from the novel. Signed lower right. Collection: Myr.

57. *The Ceremony of the Fastest Horse,* a.k.a. *Over the Prairie Fled White Otter with His Stolen Bride,* sixth of nine color prints from the novel. Signed lower right. Collection: Myr.

58. *The Fire Eater Raised His Arms to the Thunder Bird,* a.k.a. *The Fire Eater Raised His Arms Heavenward,* seventh of nine color prints from the novel. Signed lower right. Collections: Myr, Gil.

59. *The Rushing Red Lodges Passed through the Line of the Blue Soldiers,* a.k.a. *White Otter Led the Charge,* eighth of of nine color prints from the novel. Signed lower right. Collection: Myr.

60. *He Made His Magazine Gun Blaze until Empty,* a.k.a. *White Otter at Bay Emptied His Magazine Gun,* ninth of nine color prints from the novel. Signed lower right. Collection: Myr.

61. *A Monte Game at the Southern Ute Agency,* a.k.a. *Mexican Monte,* published in double-page black-and-white spread in *Collier's Weekly* 4/20/1901. Also as black-and-white "artist's proof" on pebbled art paper, 19″ × 26″ with self-borders, offered in the 1906 *Collier's* catalog of prints for one dollar. Image is 12⅛″ × 19¾″. Signed lower left: Ignacio—Col [the site of the Southern Ute Agency]. Beneath is handwritten, "Compliments of Collier's Weekly." Collections: RAM, LoC.

62. *Trout Fishing in Canada—Brought to the Landing Net,* a.k.a. *The Landing Net,* published in full-page black and white in *Collier's Weekly* 8/3/1901. Image is 8¾″ × 13¼″; paper is 11″ × 15½″. Signed lower right, 1901. Collection: ACM.

63. *Killing a Cattle Thief,* a.k.a. *At Last,* published as a double-page black-and-white spread in *Collier's Weekly* 9/7/1901. Also as a black-and-white "artist's proof" on pebbled art paper, 19″ × 26″ with self-border, offered in the 1906 *Collier's* catalog for one dollar. Image is 12⅛″ × 19⅞″. Signed lower right. Collections: LoC, StL.

64. *The Cowpuncher,* a.k.a. *No More He Rides,* published as black-and-white cover on *Collier's Weekly* 9/14/1901. Also as black-and-white "artist's proof," 13" × 9" on pebbled art paper and 20" × 14" overall with self-borders, offered in 1906 *Collier's* catalog for seventy-five cents. Also 1907 *Collier's* portfolio *Eight Pictures in Color* includes this one by Remington, among others. Signed from shadow in the foreground. Collections: Gil, StL.

65. *A Post Office in the "Cow Country,"* a.k.a. *Latest News,* published as a double-page black-and-white spread in *Collier's Weekly* 10/5/1901. Also as black-and-white "artist's proof," image 12¼" × 19⅜" on pebbled art paper and 19" × 26" overall with self-borders, offered in 1906 *Collier's* catalog for one dollar. Signed lower right. Collection: LoC.

66. *Calling the Moose,* a.k.a. *Calling to the Moose,* a.k.a. *Calling to Death,* published in full-page black and white in *Collier's Weekly* 10/12/1901. Originally offered in sepia, image 8" × 13" on paper 12" × 16½" with title below. Also an "artist's proof" in full color, image 12" × 18" printed on pebbled art paper and mounted on board 22" × 28". Offered in 1906 and 1907 *Collier's* catalogs for one dollar. Offered in 1910 catalog with same image and price but on plate-marked mount 20" × 26". Also in an edition of *Twenty-five Art Pictures Representing the Best Work of America's Greatest Artists,* published by Collier, not dated, 12" × 16½". Signed lower left. Collections: Nor, StL, RAM, ACM, Sam.

67. *A Cheyenne Buck,* a.k.a. *An Indian Brave,* a.k.a. *A Black-foot Brave,* first of eight pastels reproduced in full color as lithographs, page size 20" × 15", in *A Bunch of Buckskins,* a portfolio published by R. H. Russell in 1901.

The first four prints are Indian-related subjects and were also published in 1901 as a portfolio titled *Indians.* Signed lower right, 1901. Collections: Buf, Gil, RAM, ACM.

68. *A Sioux Chief,* a.k.a. *A War Chief,* second of eight prints from same portfolio. Signed lower right. Collections: Buf, Gil, StL, RAM, ACM.

69. *A Breed,* a.k.a. *An Indian Scout,* a.k.a. *A North-west Half Breed,* third of eight prints from the same portfolio. Signed lower right, 1901. Collections: Buf, Gil, StL, RAM, ACM.

70. *Old Ramon,* also with *A Mexican Half-Breed* added, fourth of eight prints from the same portfolio. Signed lower right. Collections: Buf, Gil, StL, RAM, ACM.

71. *A Cavalry Officer,* fifth of eight prints from same portfolio. The latter four were also printed in a portfolio titled *Rough Riders.* The term originally referred to civilian horsemen of the frontier rather than to Teddy Roosevelt's regiment in Cuba. Signed lower right. Collections: Buf, Gil, StL, RAM, ACM.

72. *An Army Packer,* a.k.a. *A Regular,* sixth of eight prints from the same portfolio. Signed lower right center. Collections: Buf, Gil, StL, RAM, ACM.

73. *An Arizona Cowboy,* seventh of eight prints from the same portfolio. Signed lower center, 1901. Collections: Buf, Gil, StL, RAM, ACM.

74. *A Trapper,* a.k.a. *An Old Time Trapper,* last of eight prints from the same portfolio. Signed lower right. Collections: Buf, Gil, StL, RAM, ACM.

75. *Caught in the Circle,* published in full

color as a double-page spread in *Collier's Weekly* 12/7/1901. Also in full-color "artist's proof" printed on heavy paper, image 12" × 18" mounted on board 22" × 28" and offered in 1906 and 1907 *Collier's* catalogs for $1.50. Offered in 1910 catalog at same price, but image 12" × 17" on plate-marked mount 20" × 26". Also issued as a miniature reproduction, 3¾" × 5½", copyright 1906. Also re-copyrighted 1908 and included in envelope with paper label as part of *Remington's Four Best Paintings.* Image trimmed to 10¾" × 15½" to emphasize central action and mounted on board 15" × 20" with corner card simulating Remington's ink signature. Also reissued in 1912 as part of *Frederic Remington's Paintings* in envelope with simulated signature on label. Signed lower right, 1900. Collections: Sam, LoC, Gil, StL, ACM.

76. *The Last Stand,* black-and-white print, paper size 14" × 15", one of four published by the Smith & Wesson Arms Company in 1902 and sold individually. Also used on retail advertising posters. Signed lower left. Collection: S&W.

77. *With the Wolfhounds,* a.k.a. *Coursing Wolves with Greyhounds,* black-and-white print with blue tone, paper size 14¼" × 13½", from S&W. Also used as advertisement in *Harper's Monthly* magazine, December 1902. Signed lower left. Collections: S&W, Sam.

78. *Hands Off,* green and black, size 14" × 16", a rare S&W print. Signed lower right. Collection: S&W.

79. *A Critical Moment,* similar size as above, from S&W. Signed lower right. Collection: S&W.

80. *The Cow Boy,* one of four full-color litho-

graphs, paper size 16″ × 12″, published by Charles Scribner's Sons 1902 and sold boxed as *Western Types.* Also published 7½″ × 5″ and matted. Signed lower right. Collections: Roc, ACM, RAM.

81. *The Cossack Post (Cavalryman),* second of four prints from Scribner's. Signed lower left. Collections: Roc, RAM.

82. *The Scout,* third of four prints from Scribner's. Signed lower left in red. Collections: Roc, RAM.

83. *The Half-Breed,* last of four prints from Scribner's. Signed lower right. Collections: Roc, LoC.

84. *His First Lesson,* published as a full-color double-page spread in *Collier's Weekly* 9/26/1903. Also as a full-color "artist's proof" with image on heavy plate paper, 12″ × 18″, mounted on board 22″ × 28″, and offered in 1906 *Collier's* catalog for $1.50. Also in 1910 catalog, same image and price but on plate-marked mount 20″ × 26″. Also re-copyrighted 1908 and included in set, *Remington's Four Best Paintings.* Image cropped to 10¾″ × 15½″ and mounted on board 15″ x 20″ with 4″ × 3¼″ corner card that said "Artist's Proof" and bore a simulated ink signature and simulated handwritten title. Signed lower right, copyright 1903. Collections: Sam, StL, RAM, ACM.

85. *The Fight for the Water Hole,* published as a full-color double-page spread in *Collier's Weekly* 12/5/1903. Also a full-color "artist's proof" with 10½″ × 15½″ image on heavy plate paper and mounted on board 22″ × 28″. Offered in 1906 *Collier's* catalog for $1.50. Also offered in 1907 catalog with 1903 copyright. Also in 1910 catalog, image 12″ × 17″ on plate-marked mount 20″ × 26″. Print also

copyrighted 1908, but not listed as such in portfolios. Signed lower right in generic *Collier's* form. Collections: Sam, Gil, StL, RAM.

86. *The Creek Indian,* a.k.a. *The Indian Head,* published in full color as *Collier's Weekly* cover 12/12/1903. Full-color "artist's proof" was mounted on board and matted to 16″ × 13″. Offered in 1906 *Collier's* catalog for seventy-five cents, size 10″ × 7⅞″. Also used as decoration for cover of small-size 1904 *Remington Portfolio of Drawings.* Signature is catercorner lower right. Collection: LoC.

87. *The Pioneers,* published as a full-color double-page *Collier's Weekly* spread 2/13/1904. Full-color "artist's proof" with image 11″ × 16″ mounted on board 22″ × 28″ offered in 1906 *Collier's* catalog for $1.50. Also in 1910 catalog, 12″ × 17″ image on 20″ × 26″ plate-marked mount. Also 5″ × 7½″ on soft mat in small 1904 portfolio. Signed lower right. Collections: StL, ACM.

88. *The Santa Fe Trade,* published as full-color double-page *Collier's Weekly* spread 3/12/1904. Also as full-color "artist's proof" with image cropped to 11″ × 16″ on heavy paper and mounted on board 22″ × 28″. Offered in 1906 *Collier's* catalog for $1.50. Also 5″ × 7½″ on soft mat in small 1904 portfolio. Signed lower right. Collections: StL, Gil.

89. *The Gathering of the Trappers,* a.k.a. *Trappers Going to the Rendezvous,* a.k.a. *The Rendezvous,* published as a full-color double-page *Collier's Weekly* spread 4/16/1904. Full-color 11″ × 16″ image on heavy paper mounted on 22″ × 28″ board offered in *Collier's* 1906 catalog for $1.50. Also in 1910 catalog, image 12″ × 17″ on plate-marked mount 20″ × 26″. Also featured on 5″ × 7½″ soft mat in small 1904 portfolio as *Trappers*

Going to the Rendezvous. Also in 1906 portfolio *Six Remington Paintings in Colors,* image 12¼″ × 18¼″ on heavy paper, size 17½″ × 23½″ with self-borders and separate 2¾″ × 4″ corner card reading "Artist's Proof/ Frederic Remington" with title. Also in 1912 manila envelope as *The Rendezvous* in second issue of *Frederic Remington's Paintings* with paper label simulating Remington's signature in ink, image about 8½″ × 12½″ on soft mat 13¼″ × 18¼″ with corner card also simulating signature. Signed lower right. Collections: Sam, StL, RAM, ACM.

90. *The Emigrants,* published as a full-color double-page *Collier's Weekly* spread 5/14/1904. Also as full-color "artist's proof," 10″ × 17″, mounted on board 22″ × 28″ and offered in 1906 *Collier's* catalog for $1.50. Also in 1910 catalog, image 12″ × 18″ on plate-marked mount 20″ × 26″. Also 5″ × 7½″ on soft mat in small 1904 portfolio. Also in 1906 portfolio as one of *Six Remington Paintings in Colors,* image 12″ × 18″ on plate paper, 17½″ × 23½″ with self-border and separate corner card reading "Artist's Proof." Also in same portfolio reissued in 1908. Signed lower right in red. Collections: Sam, StL, RAM, ACM, Cow.

91. *A Night Attack on a Government Wagon Train,* published as a full color double-page *Collier's Weekly* spread 6/11/1904. Full-color "artist's proof" with 10″ × 17″ image mounted on 22″ × 28″ board offered by *Collier's* for $1.50. Also 5″ × 7½″ on soft mat in 1904 small portfolio. Signed lower right. Collection: RAM.

92. *Drifting before the Storm,* published as a full-color double-page *Collier's Weekly* spread 7/9/1904. Full-color "artist's proof" with image 12″ × 18″ mounted on board 22″ × 28″ also offered by *Collier's* for $1.50. Also

5″ × 7½″ on soft mat in small 1904 portfolio. Signature is pale brown lower left. Collections: RAM, StL, ACM.

93. *The Bell Mare*, a.k.a. *In the Enemy's Country*, published as a full-color double-page *Collier's Weekly* spread 8/13/1904. Also as full-color "artist's proof," copyright 1903, with 16″ × 11″ image mounted on 28″ × 22″ board and offered by *Collier's* for $1.50. Also 7½″ × 5″ on soft mat in small 1904 portfolio. Also in 1906 portfolio *Six Remington Paintings in Colors*, image 19″ × 12¾″ on heavy paper, 23½″ × 17½″ with self-borders and separate corner card marked "Artist's Proof." Also part of same portfolio reissued in 1908. Signed lower center, copyright 1903. Collections: Sam, StL, RAM, ACM.

94. *The Stampede*, a.k.a. *A Change of Ownership*, published as a full-color double-page *Collier's Weekly* spread 9/10/1904. Full-color "artist's proof," copyright 1903, with 11″ × 16¾″ image mounted on 22″ × 28″ board also offered in both 1906 and 1907 *Collier's* catalogs for $1.50. Offered also in 1910 catalog, image 12″ × 18″ on plate-marked mount 20″ x 26″. Also 5″ × 7½″ on soft mat in small 1904 portfolio. Signed lower right, copyright 1903. Collections: StL, Gil.

95. *Pony Tracks in the Buffalo Trail*, published as a full-color double-page *Collier's Weekly* spread 10/8/1904. Also as a full-color "artist's proof," copyright 1904, with image 10″ × 17″ mounted on board 22″ × 28″ and offered in *Collier's* catalog for $1.50. Also 5″ × 7½″ on soft mat in small 1904 portfolio. Also in 1906 portfolio *Six Remington Paintings in Colors*, 11″ × 19″ image on paper measuring 17½″ × 23½″ with self-borders and separate corner card reading "Artist's Proof." Also in same 1906 portfolio reissued in 1908. Signed lower right in red. Collections: Sam, StL, RAM, ACM.

96. *Trailing Texas Cattle*, published as a full-color double-page *Collier's Weekly* spread 11/12/1904. Full-color "artist's proof" with image 10″ × 17″ mounted on board 22″ × 28″ and offered for $1.50 in 1906 *Collier's* catalog. Also 5″ × 7½″ on soft mat in small 1904 portfolio. Also in 1908 portfolio *Six Remington Paintings in Colors* with paper "Artist's Proofs" label. Image 11¼″ × 19¼″ on paper 17½″ × 23½″ with self-borders. Substituted for *The Gathering of the Trappers* in the 1906 issue of the same portfolio. Signed lower right in red. Collections: Sam, Gil, RAM, ACM.

97. *The End of the Day*, published as a full-color double-page *Collier's Weekly* spread 12/17/1904. Full-color 11″ × 16″ "artist's proof" mounted on 22″ × 28″ board offered in 1906 *Collier's* catalog for $1.50. Signed lower right. Collections: RAM, ACM.

98. *An Argument with the Town Marshal*, published as a full-color double-page *Collier's Weekly* spread 2/11/1905. Also as full-color "artist's proof" with image 11″ × 16″ mounted on board 22″ × 28″ and offered in 1906 *Collier's* catalog for $1.50. Offered in 1910 catalog, image 12″ × 17″ on plate-marked mount 20″ × 26″. Also in 1906 portfolio, *Six Remington Paintings in Colors*, image 12¼″ × 18½″ on paper 17½″ × 23½″ with self-borders and corner card reading "Artist's Proof." Also reissued in 1908 in same portfolio. Signed lower right. Collections: Sam, Gil, StL, RAM, Cow, ACM.

99. *The Chieftain*, a.k.a. *Indian on Horse*, published as full-color *Collier's Weekly* cover of the Remington Number 3/18/1905. Special mounted and matted 8″ × 10″ edition of the cover printed on heavy coated paper was offered in same issue for one dollar. Offer repeated 5/6/1905. Also full-color "artist's proof" with image 11″ × 16″ mounted and matted to 15″ × 20″ offered in 1906 *Collier's* catalog for seventy-five cents. Signed lower right in blue. Collection: RAM.

100. *An Evening on a Canadian Lake*, published as full-color double-page *Collier's Weekly* spread in the Remington Number. "Splendid press proof" in full color, 15″ × 21″ with self-borders, advertised in same issue for two dollars, mailed in a tube. Also included with five proofs by other artists in *Six Modern Masters* in 1906. Also full-color "artist's proof" with image 11″ × 16″ mounted on board 22″ × 28″ and offered in 1906 and 1907 *Collier's* catalogs for $1.50. Offered in 1910 catalog, image 12″ × 18″ on plate-marked mount 20″ × 26″. Also re-copyrighted in 1908, presented in manila envelope with paper label as part of *Remington's Four Best Paintings* series, image 10⅜″ × 15⅛″ mounted on board 15″ × 20″ with corner card reading "Artist's Proof" with a simulated ink signature and simulated handwritten title. Also in 1908 reissue of same envelope with different contents. The cropped print bears the generic signature lower right. Collections: Sam, Gil, LoC, StL, ACM.

101. *A Reconnaissance*, a.k.a. *A Reconnaissance in the Moonlight*, published as a full-color double-page spread in *Collier's Weekly* 4/8/1905 (copyright 1902). Full-color "artist's proof," copyright 1905, with image 11″ × 16″ mounted on board 22″ × 28″ offered in 1906 *Collier's* catalog for $1.50. Signed lower right in red, copyright 1902. Collection: RAM.

102. *An Old Story in a New Way*, published as a full-color double-page *Collier's Weekly* spread 5/13/1905. Full-color "artist's proof" with image 10″ × 17″ mounted on board 22″

× 28″ offered in 1906 *Collier's* catalog for $1.50. No signature visible. Collection: Roc.

103. *The Buffalo Runners,* published as a full-color double-page *Collier's Weekly* spread 6/17/1905. Also as full-color "artist's proof" with image 10″ × 17″ mounted on board 22″ × 28″ and offered in 1906 *Collier's* catalog for $1.50. Offered in 1910 catalog, image 11″ × 18″ on plate-marked mount 20″ × 26″. Also in 1906 portfolio *Six Remington Paintings in Colors,* image 10½″ × 18″ on paper 17½″ × 23½″ with self-borders and corner card reading "Artist's Proof." Also in 1908 reissue of same portfolio. Signed lower right in red. Collections: Sam, Gil, StL, RAM, ACM.

104. *An Early Start for Market,* a.k.a. *On the Road to Market,* published as a full-color double-page *Collier's Weekly* spread 7/15/1905. Also full-color "artist's proof" with image 11″ × 16″ mounted on board 22″ × 28″ and offered in 1906 *Collier's* catalog at $1.50. Signed lower right. Collection: RAM.

105. *Coming to the Call,* published as full-color double-page *Collier's Weekly* spread 8/19/1905. Also full-color "artist's proof" with image 12″ × 18″ mounted on board 22″ × 28″ offered in 1906 and 1907 *Collier's* catalogs for $1.50. Offered in 1910 catalog but on 20″ × 26″ plate-marked mount. Also re-copyrighted in 1908 as part of manila envelope entitled *Remington's Four Best Paintings.* Image 10¾″ × 15½″ mounted on board 15″ × 20″ with corner card reading "Artist's Proof" and bearing simulated ink signature and simulated handwritten title. Also in an edition of *Twenty-five Art Pictures Representing the Best Work of America's Greatest Artists,* published by Collier, no date. Signed lower left. Collections: Sam, StL, RAM, ACM.

106. *A Halt in the Wilderness,* published 9/23/1905 as a green-and-black double-page *Collier's Weekly* spread. Two-color "artist's proof" with image 11″ × 16″ mounted on board 22″ × 28″ offered in 1906 *Collier's* catalog for $1.50. Signed lower right. Collection: RAM.

107. *Hernando De Soto,* published 11/11/1905, full color, full page, in *Collier's Weekly.* No print was made of *Cabeca de Vaca,* first in the *Great American Explorers* series. *De Soto* was the second, a full-color reproduction, image 8¾″ × 12½″. Signed lower right in reeds. Collection: Gil.

108. *The Expedition of Francisco Coronado,* published full color, full page in *Collier's Weekly* 12/9/1905. Full-color print, image 8¾″ × 12¼″. Signed lower right. Collection: Gil.

109. *Radisson and Groseilliers,* a.k.a. *Exploring the Lakes,* published full color, full page in *Collier's Weekly* 1/13/1906. Full-color print 9″ × 13″ on paper 13¾″ × 18½″ with self-borders. Also in the 1907 portfolio *Frederic Remington Four Pictures,* same sizes. Signed lower left. Collections: Sam, LoC, StL, RAM, ACM.

110. *La Salle,* published in full color on full page in *Collier's Weekly* 2/10/1906. Image 8″ × 11¾″. Signed lower right. Collection: Gil.

111. *La Verendrye,* published in full color on full page, *Collier's Weekly* 3/17/1906. Image 7¾″ × 11¼″. Signed lower left. Collection: Gil.

112. *Mackenzie,* published in full color, full page, in *Collier's Weekly* 4/14/1906. Also a full-color print, image 12¼″ × 9″. Signed lower right. Collection: Gil.

113. *Zebulon Pike Entering Santa Fe,* a.k.a. *A Spanish Escort,* published 6/16/1906 as a full-color, full-page spread in *Collier's Weekly.* Also a full-color print with image 8¾″ × 12½″ on paper 10¾″ × 14¾″ with self-borders. Signed lower right. Collections: Sam, StL, RAM, ACM.

114. *Jedediah Smith,* published 7/14/1906 as a full-color, full-page spread in *Collier's Weekly.* Also as full-color print with image 8½″ × 12½″. Signed lower right. Collection: Gil.

115. *The Unknown Explorers,* original copyright 1904, published 8/11/1906 as full-color *Collier's Weekly* cover in heavily cropped version. Also as a full-color print 7¼″ × 5″ on 11″ × 7¾″ plate-marked mount to simulate mat. Also in small 1904 portfolio. Signed lower right in red. At lower left is the notice, "Copyright 1904 by Collier's Weekly." Collections: Sam, ACM.

116. *The Guard of the Whiskey Traders,* published 9/22/1906 as a full-color, full-page spread in *Collier's Weekly.* Also a full-color print, image 12½″ × 8¾″ on paper with self-borders. Signed lower right. Collection: Gil.

117. *The Parley,* published 10/29/1906 as a full-color, full-page spread in *Collier's Weekly.* Also as full-color print, image 7¾″ × 12″ on heavy paper 13¾″ × 18½″ with self-borders. Also in 1907 portfolio, *Frederic Remington Four Pictures,* same sizes. Signed lower right, copyright 1906. Collections: Sam, StL, ACM.

118. *Lumber Camp at Night,* a.k.a. *The Tragedy of the Trees, Part I,* published 11/10/1906 as a full-color, full-page spread in *Collier's Weekly.* Also a full-color print, image 12″ ×

8¾″ on paper with self-borders. Signed lower right. Collection: Gil.

119. *Snaking Logs to the Skidway,* a.k.a. *The Tragedy of the Trees, Part II,* published 12/8/1906 as a full-color, full-page spread in *Collier's Weekly.* Also a full-color print, image 12″ × 8¾″ on paper with self-borders. Signed lower right. Collection: Gil.

120. *Hauling Logs to the River,* a.k.a. *The Tragedy of the Trees, Part III,* published 1/12/1907 as a full-color, full-page spread in *Collier's Weekly.* Also a full-color print, image 12″ × 8¾″ on paper with self-borders. Signed lower right in blue. Collection: Gil.

121. *The Howl of the Weather,* a.k.a. *The Squall,* published 2/16/1907 as full-page, full-color spread in *Collier's Weekly.* Full-color "artist's proof" with image 11″ × 18″ mounted on board 22″ × 28″ offered in 1907 *Collier's* catalog for $1.50. Also offered in 1910 catalog, image 12″ × 18″ on plate-marked mount 20″ × 26″. Also in 1907 portfolio *Frederic Remington Four Pictures,* image 8¾″ × 13″ on paper 13¾″ × 18½″ with self-borders. Also in 1912 manila envelope with second issue of *Frederic Remington's Paintings.* Label on envelope simulates Remington's signature in ink. Sizes same as 1907 portfolio on soft mat with corner card reading "Artist's Proof" and bearing a simulated ink signature. Also in undated book, *Twenty-five Art Pictures Representing the Best Work of America's Greatest Artists,* published by Collier, including *The Squall,* same image on paper 12″ × 16½″. Signed lower right in brown. Collections: Sam, StL, RAM, ACM, Gil.

122. *Downing the Nigh Leader,* a.k.a. *The Attack,* published 4/20/1907 as a full-color, full-page spread in *Collier's Weekly.* Full-

color "artist's proof" with image 10½″ × 18″ mounted on board 22″ × 28″ offered in 1907 *Collier's* catalog for $1.50. Same image offered at same price but on plate-marked mount 20″ × 26″ in 1910 catalog, which also offered 8″ × 10″ sepia platinum prints at $1.00, 11″ × 14″ at $2.25, and 16″ × 20″ at $4.00. Also in 1907 portfolio *Frederic Remington Four Pictures,* image 8″ × 13½″ on paper 13¾″ × 18½″ with self-borders. Also in *Twenty-five Art Pictures Representing the Best Work of America's Greatest Artists,* by Collier, no date. Signed lower right in brown. Collections: StL, Gil, ACM, Sam.

123. *The Shadows at the Waterhole,* published 8/24/1907 as full-color, full-page spread in *Collier's Weekly.* Full-color "artist's proof" with image 10″ × 17″ mounted on board 22″ × 28″ offered in 1907 *Collier's* catalog for $1.50. Also in 1910 catalog, image 12″ × 18″ on plate-marked mount 20″ × 26″. Also re-copyrighted 1908 for reissued manila envelope, *Remington's Four Best Paintings,* image 10″ × 17″ mounted on board with corner card reading "Artist's Proof" with simulated ink signature. Signed lower right in gray. Collections: Sam, StL, Gil, RAM, ACM.

124. *Bringing Home the New Cook,* published 11/2/1907 as full-color, full-page spread in *Collier's Weekly.* Also in full color in 1912 manila envelope *Frederic Remington's Paintings,* with paper label simulating Remington's signature in ink. Image 8½″ × 12¾″ mounted on plate-marked mat 13¼″ × 18¼″ with corner card reading "Artist's Proof" with simulated signature. Also in 1912 reissue of same envelope. Also in 1912 envelope *Remington's Four Best Paintings,* image mounted on board 15″ × 20″ with corner card. Signed lower left. Collections: Sam, Gil, StL, RAM, ACM.

125. *The Scouts,* published in full color as the 5/22/1908 *Collier's Weekly* cover. Also as full-color print, 8⅝″ × 10½″ on mat 13½″ × 18⅝″. Signed lower right. Collections: StL, ACM, RAM.

126. *The Ceremony of the Scalps,* published 6/13/1908 as full-color, full-page spread in *Collier's Weekly.* Full-color "artist's proof" with image 12″ × 18″ mounted on board 22″ × 28″ offered in 1907 *Collier's* catalog for $1.50. Also in 1910 catalog, but on plate-marked mount 20″ × 22″ (possibly 26″), and in sepia platinums 8″ × 10″ for $1.00, 11″ × 14″ for $2.25, and 16″ × 20″ for $4.00. Signed lower right in brown. Collections: StL, RAM, ACM.

127. *The Last of His Race,* a.k.a. *The Vanishing American,* a.k.a. *The Last American,* color print on canvas, 18½″ × 12½″, published around 1908 by Brown and Robertson Co., Chicago. Signed lower right, 1908. Collections: RAM, ACM, StL.

128. *The Warrior's Last Ride,* published 11/7/1908 as full-color full-page spread in *Collier's Weekly.* Included in 1909 portfolio *Eight New Remington Prints,* full-color image 8¾″ × 13″ on heavy coated paper 11½″ × 16½″ with self-borders. Signed lower right. Collections: Sam, Gil, StL, RAM, ACM.

129. *The Grass Fire,* a.k.a. *Backfiring,* published 4/3/1909 as full-color full-page spread in *Collier's Weekly.* Full-color print 11″ × 16½″. Signed lower right, 1908. Collections: Gil, RAM, ACM, StL.

130. *With the Eye of the Mind,* published 6/19/1909 as full-color full-page *Collier's Weekly* frontispiece. Also full-color print, image 8″ × 13″ on paper 10″ × 15″ with self-borders. Also in 1909 portfolio *Eight New*

Remington Prints on heavy coated paper 11½″ × 16½″ with self-borders. Signature cropped. Collections: Sam, Gil, StL, RAM, ACM.

131. *The Quarrel,* published 8/14/1909 as full-color, full-page spread in *Collier's Weekly.* Also in manila envelope, copyright 1912, titled *Frederic Remington's Paintings* with paper label simulating Remington's signature. Image 8½″ × 12¾″ mounted on plate-marked mat 13¼″ × 18¼″ with corner card reading "Artist's Proof" with simulated signature. Also in 1912 envelope *Remington's Four Best Paintings,* on board 15″ × 20″ with corner card. Signed lower right in brown. Collections: Sam, Gil, StL, RAM, ACM.

132. *Indians Simulating Buffalo,* published 9/18/1909 as full-color, full-page spread in *Collier's Weekly.* Also full-color print in 1909 portfolio *Eight New Remington Prints,* image 6¾″ × 13½″ heavy coated paper 11½″ × 16½″ with self-borders. Title is printed below the images. Also in promotional miniature reproduction 3½″ × 5½″. Signature not apparent. Collections: Sam, Gil, StL, RAM, ACM.

133. *On the Southern Plains in 1860,* a.k.a. *The Cavalry Charge,* published 11/27/1909 as full-color full-page spread in *Collier's Weekly.* Also full-color print in 1909 portfolio *Eight New Remington Prints,* image 6¾″ × 13½″ on heavy coated paper 11½″ × 16½″ with self-borders. Signature and date cropped from lower right. Collections: Sam, Gil, StL, RAM, ACM.

134. *The Sentinel,* not published in *Collier's Weekly;* reproduced only as a print. Included in 1909 portfolio *Eight New Remington Prints,* image 8¾″ × 13″ on heavy coated paper 11½″ × 16½″ with self-borders. Also

promotional miniature reproduction 3¾″ × 5½″. Signed lower left. Collections: Sam, Gil, StL, RAM, ACM.

135. *Buying Polo Ponies in the West,* a.k.a. *Horse Muster,* published 3/5/1910 as full-color, double-page spread in *Collier's Weekly,* image 12″ × 16½″. Black-and-white print. Signed lower right. Collection: ACM.

136. *The Navajo Raid,* published 3/12/1910 as full-color, full-page spread in *Collier's Weekly,* image 8¾″ × 12¾″. Signed lower left. Collections: Gil, RAM, StL.

137. *Shotgun Hospitality,* published 9/17/1910 as full-color *Collier's Weekly* frontispiece. Image 8½″ × 12¾″, overall size given as 17½″ × 21¼″. Signed lower right, dated 1908. Collection: RAM.

138. *A Cavalry Charge,* a.k.a. *The Charge,* a.k.a. *The Revolver Charge,* the central portion of the original painting published 10/8/1910 as full-color *Collier's Weekly* frontispiece. Entire painting reproduced as full color print, image 8″ × 23″ on plate-marked mount 15½″ × 28½″, offered in 1910 *Collier's* catalog for $1.50. Signed lower right. Collections: Gil, ACM, RAM.

139. *The Pool in the Desert,* published 10/22/1910 as full-color *Collier's Weekly* frontispiece, copyright 1909. Featured in 1909 portfolio *Eight New Remington Prints,* image 6¾″ × 10½″ on heavy coated paper 11½″ × 16½″ with self-borders and title in lower margin. Neither pool nor signature visible. Collections: Sam, Gil, StL, RAM.

140. *The Call for Help,* a.k.a. *At Bay,* published 12/17/1910 as full-color *Collier's Weekly* frontispiece, image 8¾″ × 12¾″.

Full-color print. Signed lower right. Collection: Sam tear sheet.

141. *The Snow Trail,* published 1/21/1911 as full-color *Collier's Weekly* frontispiece. Featured in 1909 portfolio *Eight New Remington Prints,* image 8″ × 13″ on heavy coated paper 11½″ × 16½″ with self-borders and title in lower margin. Also in 3½″ × 5½″ promotional miniature reproduction, copyright 1909. Signed lower left in brown. Collections: Sam, Gil, StL, RAM, ACM.

142. *Stampeded by Lightning,* a.k.a. *The Stampede,* published 2/18/1911 as full-color, full-page *Collier's Weekly* frontispiece. Also full-color print 11″ × 14″. Signed lower right. Collections: RAM, ACM.

143. *Benighted for a Dry Camp,* published 3/4/1911 as full-color *Collier's Weekly* frontispiece. Included in 1912 manila envelope titled *Frederic Remington's Paintings,* with paper label simulating Remington's signature. Image 8½″ × 12¾″ on plate-marked mount 13¼″ × 18¼″ with corner card marked "Artist's Proof" with simulated ink signature. Also in larger 1912 envelope, *Remington's Four Best Paintings,* mounted on board 15″ × 20″. Signed lower left in red. Collections: Sam, StL, ACM.

144. *The Longhorn Cattle Sign,* published 5/6/1911 as full-page *Collier's Weekly* frontispiece. Print size 8½″ × 12½″; overall size given as 17¼″ × 23¼″. Signature lower right in brown. Collection: RAM.

145. *The Buffalo Hunter,* a.k.a. *The Buffalo Runner* [not *An Episode of a Buffalo Hunt* or *The Buffalo Horse*], first copyrighted 1908 and published 7/1/1911 as full-color *Collier's Weekly* frontispiece, copyright 1911. In undated portfolio *Twenty-five Art Pictures of America's Greatest Artists* as *The Buffalo*

Runner, image 8¾″ × 12¾″ on paper 12″ × 16½″. Signed lower left. Collections: StL, LoC.

146. *The Dead Men,* a.k.a. *The Discovery,* published 9/9/1911 as full-color *Collier's Weekly* frontispiece. Featured in 1909 portfolio *Eight New Remington Prints,* image 8½″ × 11″ on heavy paper 11½″ × 16½″ with self-borders and title in margin. Also promotional miniature reproduction 3¾″ × 5″, copyright 1909. Signed lower right; dated 1908. Collections: Sam, Gil, StL, RAM, ACM.

147. *In from the Night Herd,* published 3/2/1912 as a full-color, full-page spread in *Collier's Weekly.* Included in 1912 manila envelope *Frederic Remington's Paintings,* with paper label simulating Remington's signature. Image 8½″ × 12½″ on plate-marked mount 13¼″ × 18¼″ with corner card stating "Artist's Proof" with simulated signature. Also in larger 1912 envelope titled *Reming-ton's Four Best Paintings,* mounted on board 15″ × 20″ with corner card. Signed lower right. Collections: Sam, StL, RAM, ACM.

148. *Cutting Out Pony Herds,* a.k.a. *The Stampede,* published 2/1/1913 as a full-color *Collier's Weekly* cover. Print size 9″ × 13″; overall size given as 17¼″ × 23¼″. Signed lower right; dated 1908. Collections: RAM, StL.

ACKNOWLEDGMENTS

The first modern listing of Remington reproductions was the 1975 booklet *A Guide to Old Remington Prints and Lithographs* by Richard G. Myers of Canton, New York. We thank Mr. Myers and his daughter Joan Barrick.

Lowell McAllister, executive director of the Frederic Remington Art Museum, has been generous with his time. So has his aide, Mark VanBenschoten.

We are also appreciative of help from Anne Morand, curator of art, the Thomas Gilcrease Museum; Jerry L. Kearns, reference specialist, Prints and Photographs Division, the Library of Congress; Lynn Ekfelt, curator, Special Collections, the Owen D. Young Library, St. Lawrence University; George Raica and Mimi Van Deusen, the Richard F. Brush Art Gallery, St. Lawrence University; Karen N. DePonceau Flint, registrar, the Rockwell Museum; Marcia Preston and Ed Muno, the National Cowboy Hall of Fame and Western Heritage Center; Peter Hassrick, director, Melissa Webster, assistant curator, and Elizabeth Holmes, registrar, the Buffalo Bill Historical Center; Nancy Wynne, librarian, and Anne Adams, registrar, the Amon Carter Museum.

Also Jerry M. Bloomer, the R. W. Norton Art Gallery; Susan Cole, Sotheby's; Joan L. Silby, Swann Galleries, Inc.; Jerry L. Teale, media specialist, the University of New Mexico; Art Jacobson, Albuquerque, New Mexico; Carl's Darkroom, Albuquerque; Ronald Coburn, president, Savage Industries; Ellen Miller, inter-library loan technician, Archives of American Art; Tom Noeding, Bent Gallery; Jeff Dykes; Margolis and Moss; Rudy H. Turk, director, Arizona Art Collections, Arizona State University; Lee Karpiscak, curator of collections, the Museum of Art, University of Arizona; Linda Wilhelm, the Museum of Fine Arts, Houston; Walt Reed; Frank Oppel; Joan Wright.

Also Donald H. Dyal, head, Special Collections, the Sterling G. Evans Library, Texas A&M University; Eleanor M. Gehres, manager, Western History Department, Denver Public Library; Robert I. Hass, senior vice president, and Michael Shypula, director, Advertising & Promotions, Smith & Wesson; Sharon Polignano, executive secretary, Gordon Gund; Mauro Montoya; William B. Walker, chief librarian, the Thomas J. Watson Library, the Metropolitan Museum of Art; David Combs, Office of Special Collections, the New York Public Library.

Also Bob Rockwell, Rockwell Gallery; the *Maine Antique Digest,* Paul Coon, Robin Grant, William H. Kass, Joyce Driscoll, L. D. Liskin, John Glick, Frederica Hodson, and D. J. Ronald Stewart.

PHOTOGRAPHIC CREDITS

The Amon Carter Museum: Plates 1, 4, 24, 25, 26, 27, 51, 62, 135

Jack Ruddy, Albuquerque, N.M.: Plates 2, 7, 8, 89, 93, 95, 96, 103, 113, 115, 117, 121, 128, 134, 140, 141, 146

The Library of Congress: Plates 3, 5, 9, 10, 11, 12, 16, 63, 65, 86, 109, 145

Jerry Teale and Art Jacobson, Albuquerque, N.M.: Plates 6, 13, 14, 17, 19, 21, 46, 47, 50

George Gund: Plate 15

Robert Reck, Albuquerque, N.M.: Plates 18, 75, 84, 85, 100, 105, 124, 130, 131, 132, 133, 139, 143, 147

The Thomas Gilcrease Institute of American History and Art: Plates 20, 23, 28, 29, 34, 49, 107, 108, 110, 111, 112, 114, 116, 118, 119, 120

Allen Burns, Ogdensburg, N.Y.: Plates 22, 44, 45, 48, 52, 53, 54, 55, 56, 57, 58, 59, 60, 61, 64, 87, 88, 91, 92, 94, 97, 99, 101, 104, 106, 122, 123, 125, 126, 127, 129, 136, 137, 138, 142, 144, 148

The Rockwell Museum: Plates 30, 31, 32, 33, 35, 36, 37, 38, 39, 40, 41, 42, 43, 80, 81, 82, 83, 102

The R. W. Norton Art Gallery: Plate 66

Buffalo Bill Historical Center: Plates 67, 68, 69, 70, 71, 72, 73, 74

Smith & Wesson: Plates 76, 77, 78, 79

The National Cowboy Hall of Fame: Plates 90, 98

Index

For a complete alphabetical listing of paintings and their alternate titles see Appendix A.